Getting Away with Murder

The Twentieth-Century Struggle for Civil Rights in the U.S. Senate

Vanessa A. Holloway

University Press of America,® Inc.

Lanham • Boulder • New York • Toronto • Plymouth, UK

Copyright © 2015 by University Press of America,® Inc.
4501 Forbes Boulevard, Suite 200, Lanham, Maryland 20706
UPA Aquisitions Department (301) 459-3366

Unit A, Whitacre Mews, 26-34 Stannary Street,
London SE11 4AB, United Kingdom

Library of Congress Control Number: 2014943349
ISBN: 978-0-7618-6432-5 (paperback : alk. paper)—ISBN: 978-0-7618-6433-2 (electronic)

♾️™ The paper used in this publication meets the minimum requirements of American National Standard for Information Sciences Permanence of Paper for Printed Library Materials, ANSI/NISO Z39.48-1992.

Contents

Foreword

When Vanessa A. Holloway was an undergraduate at the University of North Carolina at Charlotte, she told me of her dreams to become a college professor, her keen interest in law, and she told me that one day she would write a book. I could have guessed by many long conversations with Vanessa that her book would be about the legal and legislative history surrounding lynching. In fact, I think I would have been surprised if it were not.

Vanessa has written an intriguing text on the federalism-civil rights debate, using lynching as an example, to stress that when black communities are in a calamity, the national government makes legislative excuses not to help, thus, leaving black Americans to suffer. In this case, lynching never became a federal law, but if enacted would have federally prosecuted private citizens. Although some governors sought national assistance, Southern Democrats claimed federal intervention into state criminal matters was unconstitutional. She approached her manuscript with all of the vigor and energy that I would have expected. As she was writing, I received countless emails and drafts as she delved into the subject of her passion. What results is a detailed piece of work which uses a variety of primary sources on which Vanessa builds and defends her argument that racism, not concern for states' rights, motivated the anti-lynching bill filibuster. She interrogates the motives of Southern Democrats in regard to their filibustering nearly 200 anti-lynching bills and she questions if their motives of opposition were race-based.

I have known Vanessa since she was in her teens. Just recently we met for lunch in New York City where she lives and is now a college professor. I learned that the now thirty-two-year-old Vanessa has become even more passionate about her scholarship. This was not altogether unexpected considering it is not unusual that I receive about five emails a week from her about various research interests most of which are grounded in ethics, history, and law. She has a way about her when she is excited about a topic—she gestures wildly with her hands, spills facts all over the place, and then waits for my assessment of what she has relayed to me. On this particular day, however, I noticed something more—something interesting, yet different about her. She is much more comfortable in her own valuation. She is pensive and grounded.

To the casual reader, this book will be impressive because of its history lessons. Practitioners of law, history, and political science will be amazed by the book's depth of detail and complexity. I'm sure that each time I read the book I'll be reminded that I am certainly unapologetic for having nurtured a nineteen-year-old at a time when she was coming into her own scholarship. And I appreciate that the student has now become the teacher ... and likewise.

Debra C. Smith, May 2014
Author of *The Words Unspoken: The Hidden Power of Language*
University of North Carolina

Preface

Throughout the late nineteenth and early twentieth century, Congress engaged in bitter debates on whether to enact a federal law that would prosecute private citizens who lynched black Americans. Here, the fundamental question under scrutiny is whether Southern Democrats' racist attitudes toward black Americans pardoned the atrocities of lynching. The intent is to investigate underlying motives of opposition to Senate filibustering and invite an intellectual discussion on why Southern Democrats thought states' rights were the remedy to lynching, when, in fact, the phenomenon was a baffling national crisis. Taken together, a rebuttal to this query might include notions that congressional investigations into state-protected rights deemed unconstitutional. In a unifying theme, the appeal ties into questions of the federalism-civil rights debate, noting intervals that warrant research, while advancing new perspectives intended to accentuate the matrices of race-based politics. Where appropriate, the examination underscores racial bigotry to the fullest; however, the introduction contains the best such evidence.

Vanessa A. Holloway, May 2014
New York City

Acknowledgments

Due to other commitments and responsibilities, this work has been a long time coming. The assistance of a number of people and institutions has been key to its completion. Unfortunately, all of my intellectual debt cannot be mentioned here. I do hope that those who aided me will accept this general expression of appreciation without individual recognition. I am humbly thankful to all unnamed.

Introduction

States' Rights, States' Wrongs

There is no issue in politics that is more significant than the issue of public trust. Sometimes the public do not trust government officials to act in their interest. They do not believe that these public officials respond to their concerns and many doubt their honesty.[1] Congressional inaction toward lynching was a sensitive issue for black Americans in the twentieth century, and such inaction sent a disgraceful message to them that the federal government was not on their side. By almost every measure, the filibustered anti-lynching bills were racially motivated and had nothing to do with the constitutionality of states' rights. Southern Democrats filibustered the bills because of racist attitudes toward black Americans, rather than concern for states' rights. While this argument contests Southern Democrats' legislative behavior, it also demonstrates that the anemic legal response to lynching is one of the reasons why many present-day black Americans distrust the government. In fact, lynching is only one example where when black communities experienced a crisis, the national government made legislative excuses and distanced itself from the situation, and ceded power back to the states. To prove that racism motivated the Southern Democratic-led filibuster, a few practical questions have been asked: (1) Were concerns for states' rights the core reasons for Senate filibustering, or did the argument of Southern Democrats for states' rights support the lie of racism? (2) Was the national government limited in its constitutional power to protect black Americans from private citizens who organized themselves as lynch mobs? (3) Would Southern Democrats suspend their friendships with private citizens and enact a federal law that would prosecute them for lynching? This particular question insinuates that Southern Democrats were already a part of the power structure of the South, and, as such, were friends and neighbors with private citizens who supported lynching and participated in the practice.

What is more, Southern Democrats argumentatively reasoned that federal interference was not the remedy for lynching, but, instead, the remedy was the responsibility of the states, insisting that murder was a state crime. In this matter, Southern Democrats provided ongoing constitutional defenses to validate that any federal legislative measures were beyond their constitutional authority. Provided that Southern Democrats influenced the course of the struggle, their constitutional arguments for states' rights were excuses to give private citizens the license to murder. The fundamental problem with states' rights is that, contrary to popular opinion then, policing power did not belong to private citizens. Arguably, states' rights, the underpinning of Southern nationalism, circumvented the law and were a constitutional ploy to slay black Americans. The belief that private justice was an individual's right, in which government should not intervene, was the imperfect theory that resonated with private citizens. These race-based politics diametrically opposed the correct interpretations of states' rights. It also appears safe to argue that private citizens mocked the judicial system. For example, the *Nashville Tennessean* reported:

> The mob edifies every legal restraint and makes a mockery of our boasted system of jurisprudence. It is a cankering sore upon the body politic. The mob lapses into barbarism, turns back the clock of civilization and substitutes the long repudiated doctrine of private vengeance for public punishment.[2]

According to cultural critic B. J. Hollars, some reasons why black Americans were lynched included: arson, robbery, suspected robbery, assault, attempted assault, incendiarism, suspicion of rape, attempted rape, alleged rape, rape, burglary, wife beating, suspected murder, attempted murder, alleged murder, alleged complicity in murder, murder, barn burning, alleged barn burning, self-defense, poisoning mules, poisoning wells, alleged well poisoning, insulting whites, debt, and for being black, which was no offense.[3]

Establishing such thresholds, *Getting Away with Murder* is of historical relevance as it accentuates issues of the federalism-civil rights debate. Furthermore, it revisits a penetrating topic that has disappeared from academic dialogue. The trove of scholarship enhances the argument that lynching, while cruel, was also a tool for enforcing a system of stratification, and where this system was based on the erroneous concept of race, it was meaningful for private citizens.

In the colonial era, people viewed crime as a sin, and sin, not race, was synonymous with crime. The Ku Klux Klan was founded in 1865 by ex-Confederate soldiers in Pulaski, Tennessee.[4] Lynching involved racist and sexist motivations; in fact, acts of cruelty were cast on diverse groups of people for trivial and unjust reasons. Much of private citizens' thinking derived from the biblical doctrine, "An eye for an Eye." Private citizens employed torture and humiliation not for justice, but for revenge. Revenge is not the same as justice. In the most fundamental sense, revenge appeals to the emotions, while justice is an attempt to uphold the law. To private citizens, lynching enforced local mores and punished perceived lawbreakers; in other words, it was a cultural norm. As lynching fueled social chaos, the right to private justice rested in power, as was related to a desire for control; in fact, private justice was not a reformative measure to improve society. Social equality became increasingly difficult to achieve, and this difficulty threatened society's d ecency and maturation process. No crime was ever grounds for torturing and humiliating anyone. Private citizens organizing themselves to take revenge were usually motivated by hearsay, rather than by what had actually happened; their behavior was frequently egocentric, irrational, and full of animus. In any other case, states' rights permitted angry people to acquire the sovereignty to take the law into their own hands. At worst, lynching was tantamount to a disregard of rules and authority.

In 1928, the *Chicago Defender*, a black owned newspaper based in Chicago, reported 4,951 lynchings in the United States.[5] Progressive reformers wanted to expand the role of the federal government and solve social problems. The era also redefined federalism by acknowledging federal responsibility over areas of private activity that had been unregulated.[6] A central part of the Southern legal system was the jury that never convicted private citizens. Those guilty killed black Americans with confidence that state and local police would not investigate the crimes and prosecute them. Furthermore, private citizens could be certain that a jury of their white neighbors and friends would find them not guilty. Art historian Alejandro Anreus stressed that lynching was a crime in which the guilt was so widespread that prosecution was impossible. Private citizens were rarely brought to trial or convicted of their crimes.[7] The end result gave private citizens a lynching license to personally enforce racism.[8] If black Americans wanted freedom from white oppression, the national government would have to intervene. Any new national laws protecting black civil rights would have to pass both houses of Congress. However, the problem was that every anti-lynching bill that came before the Senate faced a filibuster; thus, the Senate filibuster was the primary obstacle to black Americans' civil rights.[9] The order of society had been established and designated private citizens as culturally superior; hence, why they prevailed in getting away with murder.

Given this country's racial history, the struggle for civil rights continues to attract scholarly attention. To gain an understanding as to why a federal law to prosecute private citizens was necessary, the historiography of lynching and race relations must be examined at length. Each study's contributions aims to heighten our understanding of the federalism-civil rights debate in a distinctive and meaningful way. While *Getting Away with Murder* is a conglomeration of several ideas, the argument's underpinnings rest on secondary sources that provide an array of historical perspectives. Scholarship on the federalism-civil rights debate has its origins in Burke Marshall's, *Federalism and Civil Rights*. It was Marshall, head of the Civil Rights division of the Department of Justice, who first charged immoral government officials for the inexorable rise of crime.[10]

Political scientists Gregory J Wawro and Erick Schickler, in *Filibuster: Obstruction and Lawmaking in the U.S. Senate* covered the most ground in the briefest manner possible by asserting that democratic ideals, like minority rights, are not protected through Senate filibustering.[11] As political scientist and activist Joel Olson pointed out, racial discrimination has no place in a democratic society. In theory, democratic citizenship is inclusive of all members of a polity, while racial oppression prohibits certain people from exercising their rights as citizens.[12] Opponents of anti-lynching legislation used parliamentary procedure to prevent justice, making it difficult for civil rights activists to pursue legal recourse. Southern Democrats used the filibuster as part of their strategy for blocking civil rights legislation, however, civil rights groups made eliminating the filibuster a priority. Those who held an unfavorable view of filibustering believed that its exploitation had consequences for the process of lawmaking,[13] thus, defending congressional inaction.[14]

Further, not all believed that a federal response was the way to curtail what was happening on a local level. Even historian Frank Shay, one of the most serious supporters of a federal law against lynching, did not believe that "a federal law would stop the practice."[15] Similarly, historian James Cutler concluded: "No single statute can be enacted which will put an end to the practice of lynching; nor is it likely that any single measure can be adopted which will effectually suppress it."[16] But many did view lynching as a practice that impacted the United States in its entirety, whether or not federal law would immediately put an end to the violent behavior. Albert Pillsbury, former Massachusetts Attorney General, for example, claimed that neglect of the duty of the state to protect citizens might be declared an offense against the United States.[17] Thus, not only private citizens, but the states themselves should be held accountable by the federal government for these breaches of justice and violations of human rights. In the same way, writing in the Yale Law Journal Charles Watson opposed the ideas of Pillsbury, expressing that the government took the position that it had no liability for acts of mob violence."[18] However, writing in the American Political Science Review, David Walter redirected and intensified the debate by addressing the lynching of international foreigners when he argued that the interest Congress had in the lynching problem centered mainly on the protection of aliens.[19] Professor of Law James Chadbourn similarly noted that there was a need for Congress to take seriously a federal law that would protect aliens, but arguments against the Dyer Bill were alleged to be unconstitutional."[20] Other thinkers reoriented the focus on the rights of American citizens in new and interesting ways that continued to stress that both federal and state government were responsible for addressing the lynching problem. Writing in the Virginia Law Review, William Ford went so far as to argue that failing to prevent a lynching in the state was giving its approval to the crime."[21] Sociologist Arthur Raper discerned that in some cases, the sheriff chose not to request the aid of the guard, and, in other cases, where the guard was used, and the guard's presence was looked upon as outside interference.[22]

Political scientist Gregory Koger placed all the resources of his knowledge on explaining that the primary hurdle for black Americans was the legislative process and emphasized that the federal government had to be involved in determining what was going on in the South. The ability of senators to block bills, unless 60 percent of the Senate voted to override a filibuster, was the most problematic.[23] This is because the filibuster is not found in the U.S. Constitution. In fact, the Constitution allows the Senate to set its own rules.[24] In *Defending the Filibuster,* Professors Richard Arenberg and Robert Dove emphasized that the right to filibuster in the Senate is clearly abused. The filibuster is best viewed as a tactic of obstruction because the extended debate gives voice to minorities.[25] Sarah Binder, an expert in Congressional studies, claimed that Senators learned rebellious techniques for holding up legislation they opposed, rather than always using the filibuster to genuinely deliberate the federal government's rightful role in preventing and punishing lynching.[26] Second, the filibuster did not meet the Senate's capacity to meet its responsibilities.[27] Third, filibustering was a hateful legislative strategy.[28] More importantly, federalism provides citizen involvement in the political process,[29] therefore, requiring cooperation. Therefore, in some cases, states will partner with the federal government to deal with the issue at hand.[30] Historian Richard Ellis stated, "By creating a national government with the authority to act directly upon individuals and by denying states' rights, the Constitution and the Bill of Rights increased the strength of the central government."[31]

Joseph Zimmerman, a political scientist with expertise in federalism, acknowledged that the Constitution does not delegate authority to Congress to exercise police power, thus making it difficult for Congress to guarantee the safety of individuals. Instead, it is the reserved power of states to regulate individuals to promote and protect safety. Furthermore, the Constitution delegates powers to Congress to be used in response to particular challenges and problems, guaranteeing the nature of the federal governance system.[32] Some civil rights opponents in the Senate tried to strengthen the doctrine of states' rights and the Tenth Amendment, arguing that each state had the right to ignore both federal laws and civil rights reforms.[33] This is evidenced when sociologist Aldon Morris advanced the historical argument taking the view that southerners established a system of domination over black Americans. This system of domination protected the privileges of society and caused much suffering for them.[34]

Political scientist James Garner conceded that since the overthrow of the Reconstructionists, white supremacy had been maintained.[35] Because of that some believed that it would be up to citizens and not governments to protect individuals threatened by mob violence. Journalist and activist Ida B. Wells-Barnett frequently declared that black Americans should use violence and retaliate not only against mobs, but also against those communities that allow lynching to happen.[36] Political scientist Walter Hamm suggested that instead of using moral force to settle race relations, brute force should be chosen as the instrument for securing white supremacy.[37] According to Richard Brown, historian and former president of the Western History Association, much of nineteenth century and twentieth century violence represented the attempt to preserve whites Americans favored position in the political order and not simply as a way to enact justice.[38] Lynching became an integral part of the post-Reconstruction system of white supremacy but vigilantism arose in the response to the absence of law and order. The social strife became so bitter that order could be restored only by the governor calling in the state militia.[39] Historian Manfred Berg showed that vigilantism was attributed to the conditions on the frontier, where the people were forced to take the law into their own hands because no effective system of law enforcement and criminal justice existed.[40]

Professor George C. Wright's *Racial Violence in Kentucky*, which appeared in 1990, argued that black Americans were lynched for getting out of the place assigned to them by white society. In a number of cases lynch mobs placed a note on the body of a lynching victim as a warning to other blacks that the same would happen to them unless they stopped agitating for their rights. Most of the blacks were lynched not for rape but for being involved in politics.[41] Some authorities and community leaders urged the mob to allow the law to take its course and in cases where a black was accused of rape or murder, so-called justice inflicted by mobs was swift. From the end of the Civil War until the 1940s, black men were sometimes tried in environments where judges and juries were convinced of their guilt before hearing any evidence. In the matter of judicial lynchings, such sentences had the sanction of the law behind them.[42] Law Professor John Bessler provided a historical explanation for the cultural developments that Wright described. Like Wright, he stressed that executions and lynchings are not to be confused with one another. Whereas executions happened with the legal system's approval, lynchings were extrajudicial in and carried out by mobs acting as the authoritative figure. He went on to explain that executions and lynchings shared one truth: "At the end of the day, a human being is killed. In simplest terms, whether by the order of a judge or a group of Ku Klux Klan members in white hoods, the end result of executions and lynchings is the same: death."[43] Likewise, *Race, Class, and the Death Penalty* by historians Howard Allen and Jerome Clubb stressed that lynching was a criminal act, whether carried out by vigilantes, Klansmen, or unorganized mobs.[44]

Historian John Hope Franklin showed that fighting became a code by which Southern men lived.[45] Violence was entrenched in the Southern culture. He further argued that the prevalence of violence was caused by the South's poorly structured political entities.[46] On the other hand, historian Fitzhugh Brundage pointed out that lynching in the South during the late nineteenth and early twentieth centuries was to impose a racial hierarchy.[47] He also showed that mob violence became a type of persistence in the South. Drawing upon traditions of lawlessness rooted in slavery, lynch mobs in the South continued to execute alleged wrongdoers. In fact, lynching came to define Southern distinctiveness.[48] Brundage also claimed that the Ku Klux Klan defended the interests of the Democratic Party[49] and that private citizens employed brutal force to intimidate black politicians.[50]

Sociologist Neil Smelser examined the uniqueness of lynching in the South.[51] *Collective Violence* by James Short and Marvin Wolfgang suggested that violence based on racial and ethnic antagonisms has been a persistent feature of the history of the United States.[52] While historian and American Studies scholar Michael Bellesiles maintained that lynching was a fixed character trait of the United States,[53] sociologist Jonathan Markovitz observed that lynching was intended as a symbolized race relations and took on an array of cultural meanings. Lynch mobs ensured that blacks were aware of the strength of white supremacy and the costs of violating the boundaries of the racial order. Simultaneously, they wanted to reinforce images of white men as protectors of white women.[54] Sociologist Allan Horwitz explained that private citizens were they completely ignorant of the formal law and used practical senses of right and wrong to react to deviance.[55] On the other hand, sociologist Kathleen Blee's historical methodology portrayed the popular stereotype of Klan members as ignorant and brutal. She argued that this stereotype is historically and politically misleading.[56] Racism was ingrained in the cultural of the South. These members of the Klan found a means to perpetuate their privileges.[57]

Law Professor Charles Olgetree and Political Science Professor Austin Sarat's *From Lynch Mobs to the Killing State* made the connection between race and state murders. The work clarified that there is a long and deep connection between this country's racial politics and its uses of the killings of black Americans through lynchings. In fact, one way to track this connection is by examining the Senate's response to lynching and the Supreme Court's death penalty decisions.[58] Constitutional Law expert Gloria Browne-Marshall affirmed that black Americans have always struggled for constitutional protections.[59] American political thought expert Jennet Kirkpatrick's *Uncivil Disobedience* contended that the historical record of Southern lynchings is not always trustworthy. News sources providing accounts of lynchings were sometimes deemed "folk pornography." They existed to captivate audiences. In some cases, a black man raping a white woman was not what really occurred. Sometimes, the rape never took place; sometimes, the relationship was consensual. In either case, fiction passed as fact.[60] Historian Kimberly Harper said similarly that accounts of murders, rapes, and theft committed by blacks dominated the front pages of newspapers across the country. Descriptions of these brutal crimes carried out by blacks captured audiences nationwide.[61] Writing *Men and Violence*, Petrus Spierenburg agreed with Harper in that the Southern culture of violence was related to the slow pace of the courts.[62]

Margaret Vandiver, a specialist in the history of American crime and punishment, said, "The South was a somewhat uniform society in that its beliefs and values, devoted to white supremacy, were shared by practically all white Southerners."[63] This could be true, especially when American Studies scholar Rebecca Hill emphasized that innocence and guilt were coded white and black.[64] Art Historian Ken Gonzalez-Day acknowledged that though lynching has been thought of in terms of black and white racial categories, it also contributed to cases involving other nonwhite communities.[65] Professor of English and African American Studies Ashraf Rushdy supported both arguments by reasoning that a noose can be a symbol of automatically lynching a black male.[66] In the context of rape and lynching, historian Estelle Freedman suggested that lynching simply reinforced white women's dependency on white men.[67] In essence, lynching was a way to maintain cultural norms for both white and black Americans.

Furthermore, historian Kristina DuRocher pointed out that children who grew up during the Jim Crow South also played a role in normalizing racial violence. She contended that the cultural ideal of white supremacy was imparted to the next generation. Basically, the parents of these children encouraged their children to witness lynching rituals.[68] As Ann Gunning, American Studies, African Diaspora studies and Women's studies expert, opined mobs believed that severe and immediate retribution was the only means of disciplining an accused black man when he was alleged to have committed rape.[69] Literary historian Julie Armstrong suggested the myth of the burly black brute still plays a role in ideas about black male criminality, attesting to the power and persistence of racial stereotypes in American culture. Debates over the political and moral implications of nooses and Confederate flags proliferate today.[70] Feminist scholar Kerry Segrave made it clear that lynching began as a method of punishing suspects for alleged specific crimes. Soon after, however, lynching was no longer about supplying justice when it was not provided by the state, but it was about "power, control, terror, and intimidation"; in other words, it was about rage and hate.[71] Allen Liska's *Social Threat and Social Control* considered lynching not to be an official form of control. Instead, private citizens supported and linked with local police.[72] For the detailed accounts explaining race relations thus far, lynching was still inexcusable.[73]

Contemporary Art Historian Dora Apel's conclusion was correct to assert that racial violence was rooted in anxieties that could possibly threaten the power structure.[74] Yet, there were other ways lynching helped maintain the status quo in the South. As historian Dominic Capeci rightfully concluded, paternalists created a dependency that discouraged racial solidarity and reduced collective resistance to self-defense.[75] In *Lynching to Belong*, historian Cynthia Nevels also characterized lynching as economically motivated with political overtones. In fact, the reasons behind lynching were a combination of factors that, on any day in a specific place, violence erupted.[76] Editors Noralee Frankel and Nancy Dye's *Gender, Class, Race, and Reform* described that throughout the anti-lynching campaign, women refuted rape charges and argued that lynching was motivated by white attempts to intimidate blacks to keep them in their social and economic place.[77] Some women in the South were not oblivious to the fact that gender relations were affiliated with the racial hierarchy as well. In the same way that some scholars viewed lynching as an extralegal way of enforcing capital punishment,[78] Historian Eliza Steelwater succeeded in re-examining the similarities between capital punishment and lynching. She claimed that, "The death penalty played a role in politics in the South and West. Both legal execution and lynching, or vigilante execution, were used for financial and political interests."[79] Historian Patricia Bernstein said the same thing when she added that in the South, "Blacks were seen as an economic threat to white laborers." The lower classes regarded lynchings as a "form of free entertainment,"[80] Jennie Lightweis-Goff, scholar of English and Gender and Sexuality Studies, contended that lynching was not only violence, but was also the failure of the boundary between private prejudice and public punishment.[81] *Race, Crime, and Justice* by Professors Shaun Gabbidon and Helen Greene affirmed that lynching maintained the social, political and economic status quo.[82]

In each of their own research efforts, historians William D. Carrigan and Michael J. Pfeifer mirrored W. F. Brundage's example of state-based studies, reflecting on the histories of such states as Georgia, Virginia, South Carolina, Mississippi, and Texas.[83] Crystal Feimster scholar of African American Studies extended historian Jacquelyn Dowd Hall's research in her study, *Women and the Politics of Rape and Lynching,* to show how women's subordinate positions produced an environment that left them in danger of rape.[84] Compiling lynching newspaper articles from 1880 to 1961, Editor Ralph Ginzburg's *One Hundred Years of Lynching* provided a considerable amount of evidence detailing racial hatred to the fullest extent.[85] Once this framework was in place, other scholars added their own interpretations of lynching. An example of this can be found in the way historian Nancy MacLean treated her article on the lynching of Leo Frank. Joel Williamson furnished a psychological perspective on lynching in his study of Southern race relations. Literature and folklore scholar Trudier Harris's *Exorcizing Blackness* offered a black journalist's portrayal of burning rituals. Historian Grace Hale made witnessing a lynching a central part of her study in *Making Whiteness*, while historian Donald Mathews researched lynching as the Southern rite of human sacrifice.[86] In a final analysis, ethics scholar Angela Sims argued that mob rule developed in a society that justified unacceptable behavior through misinterpretation of legislation, which, in turn, led to lynching incidents.[87]

As evidenced of accepting lynching as a form of popular justice, private citizens were able to get away with murder. Despite the prodigious amount of popular and scholarly writing published, when the Senate filibustered on the basis of racists' motivations, it made the fight for civil rights more arduous. If it was immoral to steal, why was it not also objectionable for private citizens to organize themselves into a mob? So characterized, these accounts are useful in establishing the background for a meaningful discussion, but provide only broad models for other scholars to follow. To a significant degree, their research left room for opposing ideology; therefore, *Getting Away with Murder* crystallized what other scholars missed.

It is hoped that *Getting Away with Murder* will stimulate further research by questioning federal oversight of civil rights. The research approach is entirely analytical; it is driven by a set of questions to accentuate crimes that may have called forth private citizens and, in turn, caused their formation into a mob without provocation. This legal study is chronicled from 1890 to 1952. The selected years were carefully considered. In 1890 the Federal Elections Bill was introduced in Congress. The measure sought to protect black Americans' voting rights in the South by allowing the national government to supervise elections, but was also filibustered by Southern Democrats. 1952 was considered the first lynchless year of the twentieth century.[88] The first chapter explains how the substructures of racism was the conduit to getting away with murder. Chapter two describes how the historical root of racism was manifested into the political sphere. Chapter three are the reactions of congressmen for and against the anti-lynching bill. The final two chapters emphasize how much racism carried clout in southern culture and thus left black Americans vulnerable to private citizens who got away with murder.

NOTES

1. Joseph Cooper, "The Puzzle of Distrust," in *Congress and the Decline of Public Trust*, ed. Joseph Cooper (Boulder, CO: Westview Press, 1999), 1.

2. *Nashville Tennessean*, May 31, 1929, 4.

3. B. J. Hollars, *Thirteen Loops: Race, Violence, and the Last Lynching in America* (Tuscaloosa, AL: University of Alabama Press, 2011), 2.

4. J.C. Lester and D.L. Wilson, *Ku Klux Klan: Its Origin, Growth and Disbandment* (New York: AMS Press, 2010), 19-21; also found in Charles L. Quarles, *The Ku Klux Klan and Related American Racialist and Anti-Semitic Organizations: A History and Analysis* (Jefferson, NC: McFarland, 1999), 32.

5. *The Chicago Defender* kept track of lynchings beginning in 1882; also found in William Katy, *Thirty Years of Lynching in the United States, 1889-1918* (New York: Negro Universities Press, 1969); Ralph Ginzburg, *100 Years of Lynching* (Baltimore, MD: Black Classic Press, 1988).

6. Robert P. Sutton, *Federalism* (Westport, CT: Greenwood Publishing Group, 2002), 2.

7. Alejandro Anreus, Diana L. Linden, and Jonathan Weinberg, eds., *The Social and the Real: Political Art of the 1930s in the Western Hemisphere* (University Park, PA: Penn State Press, 2006), 156.

8. Loevy, *The Civil Rights Act of 1964*, 8.

9. Ibid., 10.

10. Richard Wasserstrom, "Federalism and Civil Rights by Burke Marshall," *The University of Chicago Law Review* 33 (1966): 407.

11. Gregory J. Wawro and Eric Schickler, *Filibuster: Obstruction and Lawmaking in the U.S. Senate* (Princeton, NJ: Princeton University Press, 2013), 6.

12. Joel Olson, *The Abolition of White Democracy* (Minneapolis, MN: University of Minnesota Press, 2004), xi.

13. Wawro and Schickler, *Filibuster*, 9.

14. Andrew J. Taylor, *Congress: A Performance Appraisal* (Boulder, CO: Westview Press, 2013), 21.

15. Frank Shay, *Judge Lynch, His First Hundred Years* (HP Publishing, 1938), 9.

16. James Cutler, *Lynch Law: An Investigation into the History of Lynching in the United States* (New York: Longmans, Green and Co., 1905), 257-66.

17. Albert Pillsbury, "A Brief Inquiry into a Federal Remedy for Lynching," *Harvard Law Review* 15 (1902): 707-13.

18. Charles Watson, "Need of Federal Legislation in Respect to Mob Violence," *Yale Law Journal* 25 (1916): 561-81.

19. David Walter, "Legislative Notes and Reviews: Proposals for a Federal Anti-Lynching Law," *The American Political Science Review* 28 (1934): 436-42.

20. James Chadbourn, *Lynching and the Law* (Clark, NJ: The Lawbook Exchange, Ltd., 2008), 118.

21. William Ford, "Constitutionality of Proposed Federal Anti-Lynching Legislation," *Virginia Law Review* 34 (1948): 944-53.

22. Arthur Raper, *Southern Commission on the Study of Lynching. The Tragedy of Lynching* (Chapel Hill, NC: University of North Carolina Press, 1933), 15.

23. Gregory Koger, *Filibustering: A Political History of Obstruction in the House and Senate* (Chicago: University of Chicago Press, 2010), 3.

24. Edward R. Drachman and Robert Langran, *You Decide: Controversial Cases in American Politics* (Lanham, MD: Rowman & Littlefield, 2008), 152.

25. Richard A. Arenberg and Robert B. Dove, *Defending the Filibuster: The Soul of the Senate* (Bloomington, IN: Indiana University Press, 2012), 2.

26. Sarah A. Binder, *Politics or Principle? Filibustering in the United States Senate* (Washington, DC: Brookings Institution Press, 1997), 3.

27. Ibid., 4.

28. Richard S. Beth, *Filibusters and Cloture in the Senate* (Darby, PA: DIANE Publishing, 2010), 1.

29. Larry N. Gerston, *American Federalism: A Concise Introduction* (Armonk, NY: M.E. Sharpe, 2007), 6.

30. Ibid., 10.

31. Richard E. Ellis, *The Union at Risk: Jacksonian Democracy, States ' Rights, and the Nullification Crisis* (New York: Oxford University Press, 1989), 4.

32. Joseph F. Zimmerman, *Congress: Facilitator of State Action* (Albany, NY: SUNY Press, 2010), 11-12.

33. Junius P. Rodriguez, *Slavery in the United States: A Social, Political, and Historical Encyclopedia, Vol. 2* (Santa Barbara, CA: ABC-CLIO, 2007), 475.

34. Aldon D. Morris, *Origins of the Civil Rights Movement* (New York: Free Press, 1984), 1.

35. James W. Garner, "New Politics for the South," *Annals of the American Academy of Political and Social Science* 35 (1910): 173.

36. Tommy J. Curry, "The Fortune of Wells: Ida B. Wells-Barnett's Use of T. Thomas Fortune's Philosophy of Social Agitation as a Prolegomenon to Militant Civil Rights Activism," *Transactions of the Charles S. Peirce Society* 48 (2012): 465.

37. Walter C. Hamm, "The Three Phases of Colored Suffrage," *The North American Review* 168 (1899): 288.

38. Richard Maxwell Brown, *Strain of Violence: Historical Studies of American Violence and Vigilantism* (New York: Oxford University Press, 1975), 5.

39. Ibid., 21-23.

40. Manfred Berg, *Popular Justice: A History of Lynching in America* (Lanham, MD: Ivan R. Dee, 2011), x.

41. George C. Wright, *Racial Violence in Kentucky, 1865-1940: Lynchings, Mob Rule, and "LegalLynchings"* (Baton Rouge, LA: Louisiana State University Press, 1990), 10.

42. Ibid., 12.

43. John D. Bessler, *Legacy of Violence: Lynch Mobs and Executions in Minnesota* (Minneapolis, MN: University of Minnesota Press, 2003), xvii.

44. Howard W. Allen and Jerome M. Clubb, *Race, Class, and the Death Penalty: Capital Punishment in American History* (Albany, NY: SUNY Press, 2009), 1.

45. John Hope Franklin, *The Militant South,* (Cambridge, MA: Harvard University Press, 1941), 13.

46. Ibid.

47. W. Fitzhugh Brundage, *Lynching in the New South: Georgia and Virginia, 1880-1930* (Champaign, IL: University of Illinois Press, 1993), 3.

48. Ibid.

49. Ibid., 6.

50. Ibid., 7.

51. Neil Smelser, *Theory of Collective Behavior* (London: Routledge & Kegan Paul, 1962), 23.

52. James F. Short and Marvin E. Wolfgang, eds., *Collective Violence* (Chicago, IL: Aldine-Atherton, 1972), 22.

53. Michael A. Bellesiles, ed., *Lethal Imagination: Violence and Brutality in American History* (New York: NYU Press, 1999), 1.

54. Jonathan Markovitz, *Legacies of Lynching: Racial Violence and Memory* (Minneapolis, MN: University of Minnesota Press, 2004), xvi.

55. Allan V. Horwitz, *The Logic of Social Control* (New York: Plenum Press, 1990), 1.

56. Kathleen M. Blee, *Women of the Klan: Racism and Gender in the 1920s* (Berkeley, CA: University of California Press, 1991), 7.

57. Ibid.

58. Charles Olgetree Jr., and Austin Sarat, *From Lynch Mob to Killing State* (New York: NYU Press, 2006), 1.

59. Gloria J. Browne-Marshall, *Race, Law and American Society* (New York: Routledge, 2013), xxxviii.

60. Jennet Kirkpatrick, *Uncivil Disobedience: Studies in Violence and Democratic Politics* (Princeton, NJ: Princeton University Press, 2008), 65.

61. Kimberly Harper, *White Man's Heaven: The Lynching and Expulsion of Blacks in the Sothern Ozarks, 1894-1909* (Fayetteville, AR: University of Arkansas Press, 2010), 17.

62. Petrus Cornelis Spierenburg, *Men and Violence: Gender, Honor, and Rituals in Modern Europe and America* (Columbus, OH: Ohio State University Press, 1998), 23.

63. Margaret Vandiver, *Lethal Punishment* (New Brunswick, NJ: Rutgers University Press, 2006), 3.

64. Rebecca N. Hill, *Men, Mobs, and Law: Anti-Lynching and Labor Defense in U.S. Radical History* (Durham, NC: Duke University Press, 2008), 12.

65. Ken Gonzales-Day, *Lynching in the West, 1850-1935* (Durham, NC: Duke University Press, 2006), 13.

66. Ashraf H.A. Rushdy, *American Lynching* (New Haven, CT: Yale University Press, 2012), 6.

67. Estelle B. Freedman, *Redefining Rape* (Cambridge, MA: Harvard University Press, 2013), 1855.

68. Kristina DuRocher, *Raising Racists: The Socialization of White Children in the Jim Crow South* (Lexington, KY: University of Kentucky Press, 2011), 8.

69. Ann Arbor Sandra Gunning, *Race, Rape, and Lynching: The Red Record of American Literature, 1890-1912* (New York: Oxford University Press, 1996), 5.

70. Julie Buckner Armstrong, *Mary Turner and the Memory of Lynching* (Athens, GA: University of Georgia Press, 2011), 22.

71. Kerry Segrave, *Lynching of Women in the United States: The Recorded Cases, 1851-1946* (Jefferson, NC: McFarland, 2010), 4.

72. Allen E. Liska, ed., *Social Threat and Social Control* (Albany, NY: SUNY Press, 1992), 19.

73. Robert W. Thurston, *Lynching: American Mob Murder in Global Perspective* (Burlington, VT: Ashgate Publishing, 2011), 6.

74. Dora Apel, *Imagery of Lynching: Black Men, White Women, and the Mob* (New Brunswick, NJ: Rutgers University Press, 2004), 2.

75. Dominic J. Capeci, *The Lynching of Cleo Wright* (Lexington, KY: University of Kentucky Press, 1998), 9.

76. Cynthia Skove Nevels, *Lynching to Belong: Claiming Whiteness Through Racial Violence* (College Station, TX: Texas A&M University Press, 2007), 3.

77. Noralee Frankel and Nancy Schrom Dye, eds., *Gender, Class, Race, and Reform in the Progressive Era* (Lexington, KY: University of Kentucky Press, 1991), 150.

78. Anne P. Rice, *Witnessing Lynching: American Writers Respond* (New Brunswick, NJ: Rutgers University Press, 2003), xii.

79. Eliza Steelwater, *The Hangman's Knot: Lynching, Legal Execution, and America's Struggle with the Death Penalty* (Boulder, CO: Westview Press, 2003), 19.

80. Patricia Bernstein, *The First Waco Horror: The Lynching of Jesse Washington and the Rise of the NAACP* (College Station, TX: Texas A&M University Press, 2006), 18.

81. Jennie Lightweis-Goff, *Blood at the Root: Lynching as American Cultural Nucleus* (Albany, NY: SUNY Press, 2011), 5.

82. Shaun L. Gabbidon and Helen Taylor Greene, *Race, Crime, and Justice: A Reader* (New York: Psychology Press, 2005), 33.

83. William D. Carrigan, *The Making of a Lynching Culture: Violence and Vigilantism in Central Texas, 1836-1916* (Champaign, IL: University of Illinois Press, 2006); also found in Michael J. Pfeifer, *Rough Justice Lynching and American Society, 1874-1947* (Champaign, IL: University of Illinois Press, 2004); W. F. Brundage, *Lynching in the New South: Georgia and Virginia, 1880-1930* (Champaign, IL: University of Illinois Press, 1993).

84. Crystal Feimster, *Southern Horrors: Women and the Politics of Rape and Lynching* (Cambridge, MA: Harvard University Press, 2009); also found in Jacquelyn Dowd Hall, *Revolt against Chivalry: Jessie Daniel Ames and the Women's Campaign against Lynching* (New York: Columbia University Press, 1979).

85. Ralph Ginzburg, *One Hundred Years of Lynching* (Baltimore, MD: Black Classic Press, 1988).

86. Nancy MacLean, "The Leo Frank Case Reconsidered: Gender and Sexual Politics in the Making of Reactionary Populism," *Journal of American History* 78 (1991): 917-48; also found in Joel Williamson, *The Crucible of Race: Black-White Relations in the American South since*

Emancipation (New York: Oxford University Press, 1984); Trudier Harris, *Exorcising Blackness: Historical and Literary Lynching and Burning Rituals* (Bloomington, IN: Indiana University Press, 1984); Grace Elizabeth Hale, *Making Whiteness: The Culture of Segregation in the South, 1890-1940* (New York: Pantheon Books, 1998); Donald G. Mathews, "The Southern Rite of Human Sacrifice," *Journal of Southern Religion* (2000).

87. Angela D. Sims, *Ethical Complications of Lynching: Ida B. Wells's Interrogation of American Terror* (New York: Palgrave Macmilllan, 2010), 5.

88. Norton H. Moses, comp., *Lynching and Vigilantism in the United States: An Annotated Bibliography* (Westport, CT: Greenwood Press, 1997), xv.

Chapter One

The Conduit to
Getting Away with Murder

There is no belief more widespread than the belief that killing people is wrong.[1] To kill a person means not having any respect for the person. Killing shows hatred and assumes a superior position over the person.[2] Throughout history lynching has had interchangeable meanings. Once, it meant nonlethal corporal punishment, then in the post-Civil War era it became to mean an open public murder by a mob.[3] Sociologists Stewart E. Tolnay and E.M. Beck defined lynching in four ways, (1) There must be evidence that a person was killed; (2) The person must have met his death illegally; (3) Three or more persons must have participated in the killing; and (4) The group must have acted under the pretext of service or justice to tradition.[4] Congressmen Leonidas Dyer of Missouri introduced the anti-lynching bill in 1918. The introduction to the bill described the mob as an ". . . assemblage composed of five or more persons acting in concert for the purpose of depriving any person of his life without authority of law as a punishment for or to prevent the commission of some actual or supposed public offense."[5] Section three of the bill outlined the federal penalties for mob violence:

> Any State or municipal officer charged with the duty, or who possesses the power or authority as such officer to protect the life of any person that may be put to death by any mob or riotous assemblage, or who has any such person in his charge as a prisoner, who fails, neglects, or refuses to make all reasonable efforts to prevent such person from being so put to death, or any State or municipal officer charged with the duty of apprehending or prosecuting any person participating in such mob or riotous assemblage who fails, neglects, or refuses to make all reasonable efforts to perform his duty in apprehending or prosecuting to final judgment under the laws of such State all persons so participating, except such, if any, as are or have been held to answer for such

participation in any district court of the United States, as herein provided, shall be guilty of a felony. Any State or municipal officer acting as such officer having under authority of State law in his custody or control a prisoner, who shall conspire, combine, or confederate with any person to put such prisoner to death without authority of law as punishment for some alleged public offense, or who shall conspire, combine, or confederate with any person to suffer such prisoner to be taken or obtained from his custody or control for the purpose of being put to death without authority of law as a punishment for an alleged public offense, shall be guilty of a felony, and those who so conspire, combine, or confederate with such officer shall likewise be guilty of a felony. [6]

The crux of getting away with murder was that there was nothing recognized then in the Constitution that protected black Americans against actions by private citizens. The Constitution pledges only to protect citizens against state government actions and not against those of private citizens. Though lynching was beyond the bounds of decency, private citizens were not held responsible for any constitutional violations. Black Americans usually suffered from private citizens' misplaced anger rather than from actual accusations. The primary method of prevention included enacting a federal law to prosecute private citizens for lynching. As noted before, racism motivated the filibuster and frustrated anti-lynching activists, which sought a federal law against lynching. Southern Democrats partnered themselves with private citizens, often taking part in lynchings, [7] and reasoned that federal interference was unconstitutional. To those a part of the power structure of the South, lynching was a cultural norm. Twentieth century politicians easily acquired positions of power and influence in Congress. [8] The Constitution does give Congress the authority to make laws for the federal government. [9] In fact, the national government can intercede when the state fails to act. [10] The primary power of Congress is that of legislation, [11] therefore, the problem of the twentieth century was not whether Congress could enact a federal law to punish private citizens, but under what conditions it chose to do so. [12] During this national crisis, it was not in the best interest of Southern Democrats, who had the power to enact a federal law, to use a laissez-faire approach to lynching. When they did resort to a laissez-faire attitude, they allowed their personal views of black Americans to affect their political decision making. Twentieth century racism in politics was deplorable and people of influence failed to show leadership to demonstrate that racism was unacceptable. [13] Senior lecturer Andy Zelleke said of government leadership, "Given the vulnerability of the societal fabric, it's imperative that people of goodwill exercise restraint and discretion in this area of racism and, most important, leadership." [14]

Throughout the twentieth century, Protestant, Catholic, and Jewish clergy, joined in demanding the end of lynching. [15] By 1924, only four states had never had a lynching. They were Massachusetts, New Hampshire, Rhode

Island and Vermont.[16] President Roosevelt was urged on several occasions to make a public appeal against lawlessness.[17] He informed the public: "The federal government through the Department of Justice can intervene and investigate situation under the federal kidnapping law."[18] A delegation of women from Southern states attended the meeting of the Association of Southern Women for the Prevention of Lynching. They demanded action from both the federal and state governments.[19] The Writers League against Lynching sent another telegram to President Roosevelt, saying: "Every lynching which takes place reflects discredit upon the federal government because of its failure to exercise its influence in behalf of justice and humanity. We strongly urge that you immediately send to Congress a special and unequivocal message demanding immediate passage of the anti-lynching bill."[20]

Lawyer and educator William Guthrie believed the Fourteenth Amendment was irrelevant to private justice, "The wrongful actions of individuals unsupported by such authority are not to be redressed under this amendment [Fourteenth Amendment]. They constitute merely private wrongs, or crimes of the individual."[21] Writing *The Fourteenth Amendment and the States*, Charles Collins explained his perception of the amendment, "So far as the Fourteenth Amendment is concerned, the Federal Government would be powerless to prevent armed mobs of whites from driving Negroes out from a state, or otherwise threatening or intimidating them in their attempt to exercise the privileges of citizenship."[22] In approaching the lynching matter, the House of Representatives, who speaks and acts on behalf of the people,[23] said:

> The states are either powerless to prevent lynchings or they do not choose to prevent lynchings. If they are powerless to prevent lynchings, then we have mob rule in the states and the violation of the constitution. If they can do it and they do not prevent it, you have a violation of the Fourteenth Amendment in that we do not give equal protection.[24]

NAACP President Moorfield Storey added the juries' role in prosecuting the guilty, "In any given case, the omission to prosecute may not be the fault of the governor nor the fault of the district attorney, but the fault of the jury. There are many cases where the authorities of the State and the grand jury have done their best only to be defeated by the action of the jury."[25] According to Editors Jessie P. Guzman and W. Hardin Hughes the remedy to lynching was not in the national government, but at the state level. "Federal Courts and officers are handicapped in bringing private citizens to justice. The state is supposed to act to bring the criminals to justice."[26] Civil rights attorney Louis Marshall confirmed that power belonged to the states to deal with lynching, "Under our dual system of Government the police power is lodged in the States and not in the Federal Government. The State has plenary power and jurisdiction to deal with this crime."[27] Law Professor Joseph Beale Jr. spoke of the states' interests, "If the law is to be carried out it must protect the state against such homicides. The interests of the state alone are to be regarded in justifying crime; and those interests require that one man should live rather than that another should stand his ground in a private conflict."[28] To remedy lynching, Thomas Nelson Page argued for additional state legislation in The North American Review:

> But it is far from certain if any change in the methods of administration of law will affect the stopping of lynching; while to remedy this evil we may bring about a greater peril. It has been tried in various states to put an end to lynching by making the county in which the lynching occurs liable in damages for the crime. It is a good theory; and, if it has not worked well, it is because of the difficulty of executing the provision. Could some plan be devised to array each race against the crime to which it is prone, both rape and lynching might be diminished, if not wholly prevented.[29]

Defending states' rights, Rev. C. O. Booth of Tennessee said, "State Rights are good as far as they work Justice, Mercy and the Fear of God. Where these are ignored, State Rights is a failure and sin."[30] Political scientist Charles Merriam offered his viewpoint of states' rights:

> Unless the legislation or administration of such a State transgresses some provision of the Federal Constitution, the National government not only ought not to interfere but cannot interfere. The State must go its own way, with whatever injury to private rights and common interests its folly or perversity may cause.[31]

Accordingly, Senator Keith McKellar of Tennessee vehemently believed in states' rights: "... I do not believe in lynching any more than does the Senator from California, but we can only uphold the laws by standing for the Constitution and for law all along the line. We are recreant to our duty when we are willing here to set aside our Constitution for the benefit of some particular or pet measure."[32]

However, the *New York Times* reported differently in that the federal courts should rule, "This federal anti-lynching bill is designed to enforce the Fourteenth Amendment. States having refused to prosecute mobs, federal courts will be given jurisdiction."[33] Also, the *Reflector*, a Virginia black owned newspaper, reported the responsibility should be put back on federal officials:

> It has been the opinion of the public for years that the illiterate whites of the South are the bloodthirsty mobsters that repeatedly disgrace this republic with this savage method of punishment; but attention should be directed now to

Washington and to that other type of mobster who filibusters and uses all sorts of tricks to give his voters unmolested privilege of burning, shooting and killing at will.[34]

The *Dallas Morning News* reported its stance on federal intervention, "If we must choose between State rights and mob violence as against Federal action and order, we cannot as patriotic citizens hesitate for an instant. As long as State law is competent and effective, then let us have it. But when Federal law is the logical and only resort, then we must call on that."[35] The *New York Times* again repeated in a different article that the remedy to lynching was at the national level, "The entire problem is bound up with local psychology and politics that action against lynchers is seldom taken, and for this reason there has been growing for years a feeling that only federal authority can meet the situation."[36] Governor Robert Carey of Wyoming clarified the scope of powers of the national government, "If the Federal Government has power to legislate to prevent lynchings, it probably has power to legislate on any matter in which Congress does not happen to be in accord with the State Governments."[37]

Virginian Thomas Walker Page argued that private citizens were not after one's race in particular, lynching had to do with criminal conduct:

It [lynching] is not against the race but against the criminal that the fury of the mob is directed. But before this fury any Negro is in one respect at a disadvantage. Suspicion falls upon him more readily than upon a white man, because the Negro belongs to the race with the larger proportion of ignorance and delinquency.[38]

Quite often petitions seeking protection from private citizens also persisted as a form of complaining:

Hon Pres & Sec of United States of America We the colored people of Yazoo County State of Miss. Do here call on you for a Separation in the State of Miss. We have no Pertection in this state it is Ruled by its Lynch law. & mob law Ever Week they is some colored man Lynch in this State and it have been so for a long time I believe if you care anything for the colored in this State you will he[a]r our cry We is Perishing in this State Please Separate us. The Govner of this State wont do anything for us. So we look to higher power. Please don't do like the V.P. I written to the V.P. & diden get any answer. I am asking for life Pertection you have herd of thoses Troubles in this State. I hope to he[a]r from you soon [sic].[39]

At the turn of the century, citizens found themselves unprepared to transition into a new era with black Americans fighting for their civil rights.[40] Racial personal disputes erupted into violent confrontations.[41] Lynching caused ongoing bitterness between black and white Americans that manifested into uninterrupted violent conflicts. Racism was the product of an unstable twentieth century society. During the early twentieth century, black Americans were on the lower levels of society working their way up, socially, politically, and economically.[42] When Professor David Camfield says, "Racism is a creation of society, there is nothing natural about it," he is correct.[43] According to Cape Town based writer Sibongile Somdaka, "Racism shapes the character of society; it pre-determines who will be rich, poor, educated, illiterate, marginalized, and malnourished."[44] Poor race relations usually caused much crime and violent encounters. Disparities between the races were because of economic differences. Despite what the lynched victim was accused of, it was economic differences between the races that produced direct confrontations.[45] Competition for jobs, not alleged crimes, generated frequent animosities. Local authorities did almost nothing to restrain private citizens from seizing black Americans from jails to be lynched. As a result of private citizens' discontentment with courts sentencing, they would take it upon themselves to torture and mutilate black Americans by setting them on fire or hanging them from trees. No private citizen was ever punished for lynching, and law enforcement, who was also usually threatened, stayed out of private citizens' way.[46] In a myriad of ways lynching sent a message to black Americans to not move into mainstream society, social, politically, and economically. If black Americans did challenge the status quo, they would be accused of a crime so private citizens could punish them with severe brutality. Black Americans were typically targeted of a lynching under false allegations.[47] The state was responsible for providing penalties against private citizens who indulged in lynching. By doing this, the state set the standard for their punishment to fit their acts. In this way, lynching would become the violation of state laws.[48]

At the federal level, the anti-lynching law filibuster debate involved limiting the national government's power and preserving states' rights to remedy lynching. Reasoning for appealing to the national government was because black Americans could not also rely on the southern legal system for protection.[49] The legal response to lynching reflected the upending social conflicts of the time. As a result of inaction at both the state and federal levels, lynching patterns became standard acceptable behavior.[50] Lynching was an example where state sovereignty exceeded civil rights. Applying federalism to civil rights issues was not a policy versus power debate. The purpose of federalism is to bring order to unsettled matters.[51] Federalism also paves the way for citizens, and in this case, anti-lynching activists, to participate in politics.[52] In fact, law professor Louis Bilionis remarked that both state and federal constitutions should be weighed together, "Federal and state constitutions thus are interdependent features of a greater American constitutional structure, the web of social institutions and practices the American people employ to articulate and effectuate their highest ideals."[53]

Despite conservative political views, Congress had the authority to create a federal law against lynching, as it was necessary and proper. The anti-lynching bills was a type of legislation that would have been constitutional, established order, and protected the constitutional rights of black Americans.[54] It seems that the purpose of the democratic system is indeed to provide laws that will protect its citizens.[55] In an unfair way, private citizens determined what was acceptable and unacceptable. In fact, the entire society decided what was right and what was wrong;[56] and for some private citizens, being in the wrong place at the wrong time as a black American was unacceptable.

Another conduit to getting away with murder was the abuse of the filibuster power.[57] It was the responsibility of the national government to not abuse the filibuster. Their intervention possibly could have prevented the over 4,000 reported lynching incidents. Preventing private immoral behavior with effective law was almost impossible for congressmen who were already a part of the power structure of the South.

All things considered, law and morals are supposed to be tightly interwoven. During this era, some foundational problems of government were close knit-friendships with private citizens. Effective governance required jeopardizing those civilian friendships to apply the law to those who violated it. To do this, law and accountability had to complement each other, but since they did not, private citizens channeled their way to getting away with murder.

NOTES

1. Jeff McMahan, *The Ethics of Killing: Problems at the Margins of Life* (New York: Oxford University Press, 2003), 189.

2. Ibid., 242.

3. Norton H. Moses, comp., *Lynching and Vigilantism in the United States: An Annotated Bibliography* (Westport, CT: Greenwood Press, 1997), xi.

4. Stewart E. Tolnay and E.M. Beck, *A Festival of Violence: An Analysis of Southern Lynchings, 1882-1930* (Champagne, IL: University of Illinois Press, 1995), 260.

5. *United States Congressional Serial Set, Issue 7921* (Nabu Press, 2012), 313.

6. Ibid.

7. According to historian Christopher Waldrep, federal prosecutors joined the Klan order; federal government employees were found to be members of the Klan; the Klan membership list was compared with rosters of government employees, and Klansmen were found inside the federal bureaucracy. Christopher Waldrep, "National Policing, Lynching, and Constitutional Change," *Journal of Southern History* 74 (2008): 593.

8. Lawrence C. Dodd, "A Theory of Congressional Cycles- Solving the Puzzle of Change," in *Congress and Policy Change*, ed. Gerald C. Wright, Jr., Leroy N. Rieselbach, and Lawrence C. Dodd (New York: Agathon, 1986), 4.

9. Ross M. English, *The United States Congress* (Manchester, England: Manchester University Press, 2003).

10. Charles R. Adrian, *State and Local Governments*, 2nd ed. (New York: McGraw-Hill, 1967), 2.

11. Ibid., 10.

12. Leroy N. Rieselbach, "10: Congress and Policy Change- Issues, Answers, and Prospects," in *Congress and Policy Change*, ed. Gerald C. Wright, Jr., Leroy N. Rieselbach, and Lawrence C. Dodd (New York: Agathon, 1986), 257.

13. "Racism in Ulster: Troubles Hid Our Prejudice; Expert Says Peace Process Has Unmasked Our Deep-Rooted Hatred of Other Cultures," *The News Letter (Belfast, Northern Ireland)*, January 9, 2004.

14. Andy Zelleke, "The Politics of Language, Identity, and Race the Rhetoric of Racism is Unfair to All U.S. Citizens, Poisoning the Atmosphere for Democratic Debate," *The Christian Science Monitor*, February 29, 1996.

15. "Churchmen Launch Fight on Lynching," *The New York Times*, December 4, 1933.

16. "Last Year Lowest in Lynching Cases," *The New York Times*, March 16, 1924.

17. "Socialists Urge Anti-Lynching Law," *The New York Times*, December 1, 1933.

18. "Roosevelt Action on Lynching Asked," *The New York Times*, October 28, 1934.

19. Julian Harris, "Southern Women War on Lynching," *The New York Times*, January 14, 1934.

20. "Writers Score Lynching," *The New York Times*, January 13, 1935.

21. William D. Guthrie, *Lectures on the Fourteenth Article of Amendment to the Constitution of the U.S.* (New York: Da Capo Press, 1970) 141–42, 144.

22. Charles W. Collins, *The Fourteenth Amendment and the States: A Study of the Operation of the Restraint Clause of Section One of the Fourteenth Amendment to the Constitution of the U.S.* (Boston, MA: Little, Brown, and Company, 1912), 20, 66-68, 72, 150.

23. Neil MacNeil, *Forge of Democracy: The House of Representatives* (New York: D. McKay, 1963), 1.

24. Segregation and Antilynching, Part II: Antilynching, 49–51.

25. Moorfield Storey to John R. Shillady, April 3, 1919 in Shillady, "Memo. in Re Mr. Storey's Opinion on Issac Fisher Brief. Subject: Constitutionality of Federal Anti-Lynching Legislation," NAACP Records, Group I, Series C, Box 338.

26. Jessie P. Guzman and W. Hardin Hughes, "Lynching-Crime" *The Making of African American Identity* 3 (1917–1968): 9.

27. Louis Marshall to Herbert Stockton, July 21, 1922, NAACP Records, Group I, Series C, Box 75.

28. Joseph H. Beale, Jr., "Retreat from a Murderous Assault," *Harvard Law Review* 16 (1903): 582.

29. Thomas Nelson Page, "The Lynching of Negroes: Its Cause and Its Prevention," *The North American Review* 178 (1904): 47.

30. C. O. Booth to Andrew Volstead, January 5, 1922, Records of the U. S. House of Representatives, Record Group 233, H.R.13 bill file, National Archives, Washington, D.C.

31. Charles Edward Merriam, *American Political Ideas: Studies in the Development of American Political Thought, 1865–1917* (New York: Macmillan, 1920), 217.

32. Congressional Record, 67 Cong., 3 Sess., 335.

33. "Dyer Plans to Push Anti-Lynching Bill," *The New York Times*, July 2, 1923.

34. "Activists in Congress," *The Reflector*, June 30, 1934.

35. *Dallas, Texas Morning News*, November 3, 1921.

36. Russell Owen, "Anti-Lynching Law is Demanded Anew," *The New York Times*, November 4, 1934.

37. Robert Carey to James Weldon Johnson, March 17, 1922, NAACP Records, Group I, Series C, Box 244.

38. Thomas Walker Page, "Lynching and Race Relations in the South," *The North American Review* 206 (1917): 246.

39. Folder 4, box 1117A, 1898–17743, Department of Justice Year Files, 1887–1903, RG 60, National Archives, College Park, Maryland.

40. David E. Kyvig, *Daily Life in the United States, 1920-1939: Decades of Promise and Pain* (Westport, CT: Greenwood Press, 2002), 1.

41. Ibid., 139.

42. "Racism: The Evil That's Not Lurking Round Every Corner; A Top Writer Puts a Social Problem in Perspective," *Daily Mail (London)*, February 26, 1999.

43. David Camfield, "Racism Yardstick: It's All about Oppression," *Winnipeg Free Press*, September 3, 2013.

44. "Time to Understand What Is Racism and Unpack Genesis of the Phenomenon," *Cape Times (South Africa)*, November 3, 2009.

45. Ibid., 140.

46. Ibid., 144.

47. Ibid., 145.

48. Victor C. Vaughan, "Crime and Disease," *Journal of the American Institute of Criminal Law and Criminology* 5 (1915): 688.

49. Ibid., 146.

50. Ibid., 150.

51. Larry N. Gerston, *American Federalism: a Concise Introduction* (Armonk, NY: M.E.Sharpe, 2007), ix.

52. Ibid., 6.

53. G. Alan Tarr, Robert F. Williams, and Josef Marko, eds., *Federalism, Subnational Constitutions, and Minority Rights* (Westport, CT: Praeger, 2004), 4.

54. Beth Walston-Dunham, *Introduction to Law*, 6th ed. (Clifton Park, NY: Cengage Learning, 2012), 59.

55. Ibid., 60.

56. Ibid., 9.

57. Ibid., 22.

Chapter Two

"No" with Authority,
the Solid South in Congress

In 1901, Representative William Moody of Massachusetts introduced the first anti-lynching bill to the 57th Congress.[1] He believed that the bill would enforce the Fourteenth Amendment, which guarantees equal protection under the law.[2] Representative Moody was elected as a Republican to the Fifty-fourth Congress to fill the vacancy seat of William Cogswell. He was re-elected serving seven years and finally resigned in 1902.[3] In approaching the issue if a federal law against lynching deemed unconstitutional, Senator Samuel Shortridge of California thought, "Senators would consider first the question of the power of the Federal Government to deal with the subject matter; then whether this is appropriate legislation, and then there would remain the question of policy as to whether this legislation would be helpful to the several states."[4] Senator William Borah of Idaho took the following view:

> We have reached a point in our constitutional history where we must intelli-
> gently consider the proposition of redistributing the power between the State
> and the national government. It is nothing less than a national disgrace to have
> a Congress constantly fighting with its self-respect on the one hand and a
> desire to meet the demands of the people on the other. And I should like to see
> this great question of whether or not we shall redistribute our powers openly
> and candidly and intelligently presented to the people. I have no doubt at all
> that, under the Constitution of the U.S. as it now stands, our attempt to deal
> with the lynching proposition would be a farce and another exhibition of
> lawlessness upon the part of Congress without anything gained in the end.[5]

The House Judiciary Committee on the Dyer Anti-Lynching Bill took issues with Congress enacting a federal law against lynching by arguing,

25

"The proposed intervention of the Federal Government directed against local power, supplanting and superseding the sovereignty of the states, would tend to destroy that sense of local responsibility for the protection of person and property and the administration of justice."[6] The leading congressmen[7] who favored states' rights were: Representative Hatton Sumners of Texas who was elected as a Democrat to the Sixty-third and to the sixteen succeeding Congresses;[8] Representative Andrew Montague of Virginia who was elected as a Democrat to the Sixty-third and to the twelve succeeding Congresses and served until his death in 1937;[9] Representative James Wise of Georgia was elected as a Democrat to the Sixty-fourth and to the four succeeding Congresses;[10] Representative John Tillman of Arkansas was elected as a Democrat to the Sixty-fourth and to the six succeeding Congresses;[11] and Representative Frederick Dominick of South Carolina was elected as a Democrat to the Sixty-fifth and to the seven succeeding Congresses.[12] These congressmen militantly counter argued for the anti-lynching bill and did not see fit to treat the matter more or at a greater length, ". . . this bill, establishing the principles which it embodies and the congressional powers which it assumes to obtain, would strip the states of every element of sovereign power, control, and final responsibility for the personal and property protection of its citizens."[13]

Other congressmen who strongly opposed the anti-lynching bill and championed states' rights included Senator Thaddeus Caraway of Arkansas who was elected as a Democrat to the Senate in 1920 and reelected serving until his death in 1931.[14] He believed, "The Dyer Bill would encourage a Negro to believe that the strong arm of the Federal Government was going to protect him and save him from punishment, however infamous his crime might be."[15] Senator William Bruce of Maryland was elected as a Democrat to the United States Senate and served for six years.[16] He firmly asserted that he would not vote in the Senate for the bill by stating, "This federal measure would be upheld unconstitutional; and persuaded that if it were enacted and the attempt made to enforce it, the result would be to irritate and inflame sentiment in the various states, so that it would do more harm than good. The remedy was action by the states to prevent lynching."[17] House Speaker Walter Sillers claimed, "Unless the reserved powers of the states are protected against unlawful usurpation by the Federal Government the states will be stripped of their sovereign powers, and will exist only as vassals subservient to the will and sufferance of the Federal Government."[18] Representative Sumners of Texas commented, "It would increase rather than decrease mob violence, and would have a tendency to engender race hatred. It would also be an invasion of states' rights and devoting much time to a discussion of the constitutional phase of the question.[19] Senator Thomas Connally of Texas was elected as a Democrat to the Senate in 1928 and reelected on occasions reelected and served for 24 years.[20] He said, "Feeling that the bill is a deliberate affront to the people of the Southern States and to all local State governments, Senators from the Southern States will resist and oppose its enactment to the uttermost."[21] Representative Charles E. Bennett of Florida was elected as a Democrat to the Eighty-first and to the twenty-one succeeding Congresses.[22] He firmly contended:

> I oppose this type of legislation because I feel that it is projecting still further the Federal Government into local government which trend in government in late years I feel to be a mistake and a very dangerous mistake. When you approach this question with regard to the South, what you are really interested in is trying to decrease the number of lynchings, I think it is quite probable that the enactment of a law of this kind will not decrease the incidence of lynching, it might increase the incidence of lynching because it will be a slap at a person.[23]

Senator Walter F. George was elected in 1922 as a Democrat to the Senate to fill the vacancy of Thomas E. Watson of Georgia. He served for a total of 35 years.[24] He similarly expressed, "The anti-lynching bill would involve total and absolute police power for the Federal Government in all the states. Our whole Constitution is a direct and intentional limitation on the power of the majority."[25] Representative William C. Wright of Georgia was elected as a Democrat to the Sixty-fifth Congress to fill the vacancy of Representative William C. Adamson who resigned. Wright was reelected to the Sixty-sixth and to the six succeeding Congresses.[26] He observed:

> It [anti-lynching bill] not only encroaches upon, but obliterates the rights of the sovereign states and seeks to substitute federal for states law, and transfer from the state to the federal courts a class of offenders for the trial and punishment of whom ample provision has already been made by laws of the several states.[27]

Senator Albert Cummins of Iowa was elected as a Republican to the Senate in 1908 to fill the vacancy of William B. Allison; he served from 1908 until his death in 1926.[28] He confirmed, "It would be very unwise and even impossible for the Federal Government to enter the State and punish crimes committed there unless it was shown that the State had abandoned or abdicated its duty with respect to certain persons or a certain class of people and crimes."[29] Finally, Representative Finis J. Garrett of Tennessee was elected as a Democrat to the Fifty-ninth and to the eleven succeeding Congresses.[30] He asked, "Do these gentlemen realize that when they are voting to put the whole police force of their city and State absolutely under the control of the Federal Government?"[31]

Aside from the congressional debates, Erle Johnston, editor of the Scott County Times of Forest, Mississippi, also supported states' rights: "We believe in the rights of the states to solve many of their [Black Mississippians] problems. We ask that we in the South be allowed to solve our own problems to the best of our abilities. We could do no more, and no less, regardless of legislation or orders from the courts."[32]

On the other hand, some House Judiciary Committee members urged Congress to exercise its congressional powers:

> It is made the duty of the Congress under the Constitution to enact such laws as may be needful to assure that no State shall deny to any person within its jurisdiction the equal protection of the laws. Within the limits of the jurisdiction thus conferred the Congress has the right to exercise its discretion as to what laws or what means can best accomplish the desired end.[33]

The Committee further said:

> We do petition Congress to pass an act so declaring, and give federal grand juries and the courts the right to indict and try these charges thereunder. Not only that, but I have other petitions to the president and the Congress begging that action be taken so that the United States courts may have jurisdiction to investigate and try men charged with this crime. If this bill is enacted into law, it will help to save the lives of human beings and to protect communities from mobs and these lynchings that have come to disgrace our republic. The Constitution of the United States gives us the authority to legislate. We brought before our committee distinguished lawyers to argue and consider the constitutionality of it. The Attorney General of the United States says the bill is constitutional.[34]

The congressmen who supported the anti-lynching bill and encouraged federal intervention included Representative Martin Ansorge of New York who was elected as a Republican to the Sixty-seventh Congress.[35] He opined:

> In many states lynchings have consistently gone unpunished. They have been tolerated, if not encouraged. To have punished the offenders would have prevented many subsequent lynchings. That is the very purpose of this bill, to grant protection by punishing offenders. By failing to bring to justice the perpetrators of lynching, clearly have states denied the protection guaranteed by the Constitution.[36]

Further, Representative Ogden Mills of New York was elected as a Republican to the Sixty-seventh, Sixty-eighth, and Sixty-ninth Congresses.[37] He declared, "I wanted the nation as a whole, speaking through its national government, not only to condemn this hideous blot on our civilization, but to do all in its power to end it."[38] Representative Roy Woodruff of Michigan was elected as a Republican to the Sixty-seventh and to the fifteen succeeding Congresses.[39] He remarked, "I naturally feel that no more worthy cause could engage the attention of Congress or anybody else than to stamp out the crime and disgrace of lynching."[40] Representative Andrew J. Volstead of Minnesota was elected as a Republican to the Fifty-eighth and to the nine succeeding Congresses.[41] He explained: "The contention that such a construction is inadmissible because it would give the federal courts jurisdiction of every criminal offense is an argument against a policy and not against the power of Congress. It is the function of Congress and not the courts to determine policies."[42]

Some news sources reported reactions concerning lynching and the anti-lynching bill. The *New York Times* reported, "There has been a cowardly fear on the part of the authorities, a criminal silence on the part of the better class of the people, and an aggressive blatancy on the part of the mob. The thousands of excuses for the lynchers by all classes of citizens show a community corrupted in civil ideals and void of civil and moral virility."[43] "Senators filibustered, they say, questions the constitutionality of states' rights. Those who apologize for lynching as a necessary defense of womanhood, the commission maintained in reality doubly betray the southern woman. First, in making her danger greater by exaggerating her helplessness, and, second, by undermining the authority of police and courts, which are her legitimate protectors."[44] "It is the duty of the Sheriff to be on the watch for any signs of lynching; it is the duty of the Sheriff to outwit and avoid the mob, if possible; it is the duty of the Sheriff to summon to his aid a posse of determined friends; it is the duty of the Sheriff to face the mob before the jail."[45] "The Congress must provide the means of ending this cowardly crime. It is in punishing those who take part in it or who permit it that Congress has the power to enact this bill into law."[46] "The South should be left alone to settle its Negro question. It is doing the very best it can, and interference from outside will not help. The good people of the South and Georgia deplore lynchings just as the good people of other states deplore them."[47] "In part, many southerners of both races have reached the conviction, with other citizens, that lynching never will be ended unless federal aid is given to the states."[48] The *Greensboro Daily* reported, "Another invasion of states' rights by the Federal Government but the Federal Government is justified in this instance, because none of the states has made an honest effort to prevent lynchings by making examples of those who indulge in them."[49] Lastly, The *Nashville Banner* reported, "This anti-lynching law would overthrow a very important prerogative reserved for the states, and would be a dangerous encroachment on the right of local self-government."[50]

President Calvin Coolidge was one of the seven presidents to petition Congress to enact a federal law against lynching. In a speaking engagement he once stated, "Congress should exercise all its power of prevention and punishment against lynching for which Negroes furnish a majority of the victims."[51] In addition to the filibustered anti-lynching bills, another bill that was not passed which affected black Americans was the Federal Elections

Bill. On June 14, 1890, Senator Henry Lodge of Massachusetts submitted the Federal Elections Bill to the House of Representatives. The bill allowed constituents to petition a federal judge to charge a national election rather than leaving the process to local southern officials. Moreover, the federal government would appoint supervisors to oversee all facets of federal elections. In essence, federal troops would monitor violent elections.[52] When Congressmen Lodge emphasized the purpose of the bill, he stressed that it was to "secure complete publicity at every stage of a congressional election."[53] But even more, he presented a case on behalf of black Americans as to why they were worthy of this kind of federal protection, "He deserved a better reward from the country, North and South, than to be cheated politically of his voting rights."[54] During this era, southerners circumvented the Fifteenth Amendment by implementing voting pre-conditions such as the literacy tests and bureaucratic restrictions such as the poll tax. Southerners also used fraud and intimidation at the ballots to prevent black Americans from voting. When the Southern Democrats also filibustered this bill, two messages were sent. First, the filibuster condoned bureaucratic restrictions and second, it legalized white supremacy in which black Americans had to endure without federal oversight to their violated civil rights. As a result of the Senate filibuster, the bill never came to the floor.[55] Although the bill would have protected black American voters from bureaucratic restrictions, the bill passed the House but was defeated in the Senate.[56] Again, even with this particular bill, Southern Democrats still favored states' rights. Some activists expressed their disappointment in news articles. Speaking of the Republican Party, Rev. R. Graham of Pennsylvania wrote in the *Christian Recorder*, "God will not let any party prosper which will not advocate the cause of justice for all men." The Republican Party also expressed outrage at the bill's failure in the same news source, "The failure of the late Congress to pass the Lodge bill settles the fact that all white is more important than all Republican to the party composing the majority of that congress." Some congressmen pressed onward to show that the party was not giving up in supporting black Americans civil rights. George Hoar, a Massachusetts Republican and supporter of the bill claimed, "The error of the South, in dealing with this problem is in their assumption that race hatred is the dominant passion of the human soul; that it is stronger than love of country, stronger than the principle of equality . . . stronger than justice . . . you have tried everything else, try justice."[57] Also showing fervent support for the bill Congressmen Lodge argued, "If it is important to protect American industries, it is vastly more important to protect American voters in their right to vote." He further asserted, "To demand honest elections is neither to raise a war issue nor is it wavering the bloody shirt."[58] Other Republican Party members stood firm in its advocacy for the bill, "We demand that every citizens of the United States shall be allowed to cast one free and unrestricted ballot in all public elections . . . the party will never relax its efforts until the integrity of the ballot . . . shall be guaranteed and protected in every State."[59] Still some others said, "The colored people are now really in a worse condition than they were as slaves. They have no protection whatever for life or property." A local Charleston, South Carolinian wrote Congressman Lodge stating, "The failure to past the Lodge Election bill has knocked us completely out in this state." He ended by determining that, "now we will have trouble to carry the black district."[60]

Since Reconstruction until the middle of the twentieth century, Southern Democrats resisted efforts to enact anti-lynching bills. They stood by the contention that such bills were unconstitutional.[61] One who remained unmoved in his opposition was Senator Lee Overman of North Carolina, when he asked: "I want someone to tell me what the purpose of the bill is, what good it will do, what it can accomplish, what can be accomplished through the Federal court if the State court cannot accomplish anything?"[62]

NOTES

1. For a profile of Congress from the 51st–82nd, see Appendix A.

2. "Public Conduct Legislation: History of Anti-Lynching Legislation in Congress," *The Congressional Digest* 1 (1922): 10.

3. *History, Art & Archives, U.S. House of Representatives*, "MOODY, William Henry," http://history.house.gov/People/Detail/18441 (May 16, 2014).

4. Congressional Record, 67, Congress, 3 Session, 13084.

5. William E. Borah, letter to the editor, *Boston Transcript,* June 8, 1922.

6. "Report of House Judiciary Committee on Dyer Anti-Lynching Bill," *The Congressional Digest,* October 31, 1921, 12.

7. For a full list of Southern Democratic Senators from the 51st–82nd Congress, see Appendix B.

8. *History, Art & Archives, U.S. House of Representatives*, "SUMNERS, Hatton William," http://history.house.gov/People/Detail/22464 (May 16, 2014).

9. *History, Art & Archives, U.S. House of Representatives*, "MONTAGUE, Andrew Jackson," http://history.house.gov/People/Detail/18415 (May 16, 2014).

10. *History, Art & Archives, U.S. House of Representatives*, "WISE, James Walter," http://history.house.gov/People/Detail/23991 (May 16, 2014).

11. *History, Art & Archives, U.S. House of Representatives*, "TILLMAN, John Newton," http://history.house.gov/People/Detail/22968 (May 16, 2014).

12. *History, Art & Archives, U.S. House of Representatives*, "DOMINICK, Frederick Haskell," http://history.house.gov/People/Detail/12339 (May 16, 2014).

13. "The House Debates the Dyer Anti-Lynching Bill," *The Congressional Digest* 1 (1922): 13.

14. *History, Art & Archives, U.S. House of Representatives*, "CARAWAY, Thaddeus Horatius," http://history.house.gov/People/Detail/10626 (May 16, 2014).

15. 63 Congress Record 400 (1922).

16. Senator William Bruce, D-MD, Senate Featured Biographies, Senate Historical Office, Washington, D.C. [http://bioguide.congress.gov/scripts/biodisplay.pl?index=B000972].

17. "An Anti-Lynching Senator," *The New York Times*, August 12, 1923.

18. *Southern School News*, May 1956.

19. "Filibuster Delays Anti-Lynching Bill," *New York Times*, January 5, 1922.

20. Senator Thomas Connally, D-TX, Senate Featured Biographies, Senate Historical Office, Washington, D.C. [http://bioguide.congress.gov/scripts/biodisplay.pl?index=C000684].

21. "Lynch Bill Faces Senate Filibuster," *The New York Times,* March 26, 1940.

22. *History, Art & Archives, U.S. House of Representatives*, "BENNETT, Charles Edward," http://history.house.gov/People/Detail/9257 (May 16, 2014).

23. "Statement of Charles E. Bennett, A Representative in Congress from the State of Florida," Anti-lynching and Protection of Civil Rights, Hearings before Subcommittee of the Committee on the Judiciary, House of Representatives, 81st Congress, 1st and 2d Sessions, June 1949; January 1950. Washington, DC: U.S. Government Printing Office, 1950.

24. Senator Walter George, D-GA, Senate Featured Biographies, Senate Historical Office, Washington, D.C. [http://bioguide.congress.gov/scripts/biodisplay.pl?index=G000131].

25. "Drive on Filibuster Opened in Senate on Truman Order," *The New York Times,* March 1, 1949.

26. Senator William Wright, D-GA, Senate Featured Biographies, Senate Historical Office, Washington, D.C. [http://bioguide.congress.gov/scripts/biodisplay.pl?index=W000773].

27. *The Congressional Digest*, March 1922, 14.

28. Senator Albert Cummins, R-IA, Senate Featured Biographies, Senate Historical Office, Washington, D.C. [http://bioguide.congress.gov/scripts/biodisplay.pl?index=C000988].

29. Congressional Record, 404.

30. *History, Art & Archives, U.S. House of Representatives*, "GARRETT, Finis James," http://history.house.gov/People/Detail/13664 (May 16, 2014).

31. *The Congressional Digest*, March 1922, 15.

32. "The Message from Mississippi: Talk Prepared for Speakers Bureau of Public Relations Department, Mississippi State Sovereignty Commission," Facts on Film (microfilm), July 1961 to June 1962, roll no. 14, N14 3635–43.

33. "Report of House Judiciary Committee on Dyer Anti-Lynching Bill," *The Congressional Digest,* October 31, 1921, 12.

34. "The House Debates the Dyer Anti-Lynching Bill," *The Congressional Digest* 1 (1922): 13.

35. *History, Art & Archives, U.S. House of Representatives*, "ANSORGE, Martin Charles," http://history.house.gov/People/Detail/8627 (May 16, 2014).

36. Congressional Record 547 (Ansorge, December 19).

37. *History, Art & Archives, U.S. House of Representatives*, "MILLS, Ogden Livingston," http://history.house.gov/People/Detail/18302 (May 16, 2014).

38. "Dyer Lynching Bill is upheld by Mills," *The New York Times,* January 5, 1925.

39. History, Art & Archives, U.S. House of Representatives, "WOODRUFF, Roy Orchard," http://history.house.gov/People/Detail/24074 (May 16, 2014).

40. "Anti-Lynching Bill," *The Crisis*, February 1935.

41. *History, Art & Archives, U.S. House of Representatives*, "VOLSTEAD, Andrew John," http://history.house.gov/People/Detail/21013 (May 16, 2014).

42. "Further Debate in the House on the Dyer Anti-Lynching Bill," *The Congressional Digest,* March 1922, 14.

43. "Priest Probed Lynching," *The New York Times*, June 29, 1903.

44. "Denounces Lynching of Innocent Negroes," *The New York Times*, November 10, 1931.

45. "Southerners on Lynching," *The New York Times*, October 8, 1906.

46. "The Anti-Lynching Bill," *The New York Times*, March 5, 1922.

47. "Calder Assailed on Lynching Story," *The New York Times*, July 14, 1922.

48. "Constigan Demands Anti-Lynching Law," *The New York Times*, January 7, 1935.

49. *Greensboro (NC) Daily News*, December 10, 1921, taken from Congressional Record, 67 Congress, 2 Session, 792 (January 4, 1922).

50. Nashville (Tenn.) Banner, December 31, 1921, in Records of the NAACP, Library of Congress, Manuscript Division, Group I, Series C, Box 248.

51. William F. Pinar, *The Gender of Racial Politics and Violence in America: Lynching, Prison Rape, and the Crisis of Masculinity* (New York: Peter Lang International Academic Publishers, 2001), 712.

52. Matthew Wasniewski, ed., *Black Americans in Congress, 1870-2007*, 3rd ed. (Washington, D.C.: United States Congress, 2008), 165.

53. Mark R. Schneider, *Boston Confronts Jim Crow, 1890-1920* (Boston: Northeastern, 1997), 35.

54. Ibid.

55. Ibid., 211.

56. Ibid., x.

57. Margaret Garb, *Freedom's Ballot: African American Political Struggles in Chicago from Abolition to the Great Migration* (Chicago, IL: University Of Chicago Press, 2014), 80.

58. Mark R. Schneider, *Boston Confronts Jim Crow, 1890–1920,* 34.

59. Stephen Skowronek and Matthew Glassman, eds., *Formative Acts: American Politics in the Making* (Philadelphia: University of Pennsylvania Press, 2008), 127.

60. Mark R. Schneider, *Boston Confronts Jim Crow, 1890–1920,* 34.

61. "Anti-Lynching Bill Up in House Today," *The New York Times*, January 9, 1940.

62. Congressional Record, 444.

Chapter Three

Blaming Racism and the Democratic Solidarity in the Senate

"Racism in politics can produce consequences."[1] To accuse someone of being a racist means that person has some kind of moral failure.[2] Twentieth century racial prejudice violated the moral demand to treat black Americans as an equal citizen.[3] Eliminating racism required a transformation of society.[4] In the twentieth century, decreasing violence was essential to progressive change[5] As a result of congressional inaction toward lynching, most of the twentieth century political decisions for black Americans were racially motivated.[6] Lynching reinforced private citizens' sense of privilege and supremacy.[7] By organizing into mobs, private citizens exercised illegitimate power.[8] Having grown up in a racist's society, private citizens harbored its racial influence.[9] This negative type of influence destroyed black communities and also demolished black Americans' dreams of equal rights.[10] For a region in which racism had been the structure for centuries, blaming racism was no challenge at all.[11]

Frederick Douglass was a well-known orator, moralist, and social reformer. As a critic, he reminded the country of its commitment to justice to all.[12] While laboring in the anti-lynching campaign, he criticized the national government for its failures:

> The Federal Government, so far as we are concerned, has abdicated its functions and abandoned the objects for which the Constitution was framed and adopted, and for this I arraign it at the bar of public opinion, both of our country and that of the civilized world. I am here to tell the truth, and to tell it without fear or favor, and the truth is that neither the Republican Party nor the Democratic Party has yet complied with the solemn oath, taken by their respective representatives, to support the Constitution, and execute the laws enacted under its provisions. They have promised us law, and abandoned us to

anarchy; they have promised protection, and given us violence; they have promised us fish, and given us a serpent. [13]

President Woodrow Wilson was also known to dislike violence, lynching, and racism. [14] During his presidency he frequently denounced lynching and more often despised racial issues. [15] In one instance he did share his personal feelings about congressional inaction to lynching:

> The question of the relation of the States to the Federal Government is the cardinal question of our constitutional system. At every turn of our national development we have been brought face to face with it, and no definition either of statesmen or of judges has ever quieted or decided it. It cannot be settled by the opinion of any one generation, because it is a question of growth, and every successive stage of our political and economic development gives it a new aspect, makes it a new question. The general lines of definition which were to run between the powers granted to Congress and the powers reserved to the States, but the subject matter of that definition is constantly changing. [16]

Lynch law was widespread in the twentieth century. Private citizens assumed it was their responsibility to take the law into their own hand. [17] Historian John Blassingame emphasized the effect of lynch law in the South:

> To whip, stab, shoot, hang or burn the alleged culprit, without intervention of courts, counsel, judges, juries or witnesses in such cases it is not the business of accusers to prove guilt, but it is for the accused to prove innocence, a thing hard for any man to do, even in a court of law, and utterly impossible for him to do in these infernal lynch courts. A man accused, frightened and captured by a motley crowd, dragged with a rope about his neck in midnight darkness to the nearest tree, and told in coarsest terms of profanity to prepare for death, would be more than human if he did not, in his terror-stricken appearance, more confirm suspicion of guilt than the contrary. There are occasional cases in which white men are lynched, but one sparrow does not make a summer. Everyone knows that what is called lynch law is peculiarly the law for colored people and for nobody else. If there were no other grievances than this horrible and barbarous lynch law custom we should be justified in assembling as we have now done to expose and denounce it. [18]

By the early twentieth century, the country was rebuilding from the Reconstruction-era a political system of white supremacy. The result of this kind of racial inequality was called the Jim Crow system. [19] Historian Walter Fleming's rendered his view of the political hegemony that was established:

> Resolved, that we hold this to be a government of white people, made and to be perpetuated for the exclusive political benefit of the white race, and in accordance with the constant adjudication of the U.S. Supreme Court, that the people of African descent cannot be considered as citizens of the U.S. and that

there can in no event nor under any circumstances be any equality between the white and other races.[20]

To escape lynching and search for safe spaces, the twentieth century mass black exodus was necessary. According to Professor Alan DeSantis:

To die from the bite of frost is far more glorious than at the hands of a mob. I beg you, my brother, to leave the benighted land. You are a free man. Show the world that you will not let false leaders lead you. Your neck has been in the yoke. Will you continue to keep it there because some white folks want you to? Leave for all quarters of the globe. Get out of the South. Your being there in the numbers in which you are gives the Southern politician too strong a hold on your progress.[21]

As part of the mass exodus, Jamaican political leader Marcus Garvey encouraged black Americans to return to Africa. He believed that racism produced a sense a self-hatred. Therefore, to remove this feeling of inferiority, black Americans needed to spiritually identify with Africa.[22] Adding to reasons for migrating, historian Phillip Foner agreed with DeSantis:

To passively remain here and occupy our present ignoble status, with the possibility of being shot, hung or burnt, not only when we perpetrate deeds of violence ourselves, but whenever some bad white man wishes to dark his face and outrage a female, as I am told is often done, is a matter of serious reflection.[23]

When he spoke about domestic affairs President Theodore Roosevelt expressed his fear of failure in his executive role and having the power to control lynching. "I should be sorry to lose the Presidency, but I should be a hundredfold more sorry to gain it by failing to try, in every way in my power, to put a stop to lynching and to brutality and wrong of any kind."[24] During one speaking engagement he did condemn private citizens for lynching and spoke of spreading peace. He reminded the country:

To bear in mind that the great end in view is righteousness, justice as between man and man, nation and nation, the chance to lead our lives on a somewhat higher level. Peace is generally good in itself, but it is never the highest good unless it comes as the handmaid of righteousness, and it becomes a very evil thing if it serves merely as a mask for cowardice and sloth, or as an instrument to further the ends of despotism or anarchy. We despise and abhor the bully, the brawler, the oppressor, whether in private or public life.[25]

To improve race relations and move toward a progressive society, the law had to be established, maintained, and fairly enforced[26] at both the state and federal level. British academic Vron Ware presented her thoughts on race separation and prejudice:

Fundamentally opposed to the system of race separation by which the despised members of a community are cut off from the social, civil and religious life of their fellow man. It regards lynchings and other forms of brutal justice on the weaker communities of the world as having their root in race prejudice, which is directly fostered by the estrangement, and lack of sympathy consequent on race separation.[27]

The conditions of black Americans in the South were such that they were not afforded legal protection. In fact blacks had, "no rights which the white man was bound to respect."[28] Anti-lynching activist Ida B. Wells confirmed, "The Afro-American is thus the backbone of the South. A thorough knowledge and judicious exercise of this power in lynching localities could many times effect a bloodless revolution."[29] Considering Wells' position, Defense Attorney Luther Rosser admitted the gaps in the judicial system:

Our judicial system is not perfect, but lynchings cannot be attributed to that fact. Whatever the faults of our legal system, it is not responsible for lynch law. The mob lynches not by reason of any defect or delay in the law, but because the aroused passions of the mob want no law and will wait for no law, no matter how certain, no matter how swift. Lynching is not a protest against law, but is the outburst of primeval passion that ignores all law, waits on no court, and is satisfied with no punishment which it does not select and which it does not inflict. No legal sentence is severe enough, no legal execution brutal enough. The mob wants to rend and tear, mutilate and bum. It will not tolerate the sheriff as executioner.[30]

When the national government withdrew its protective power, private citizens were at will to terrorize black Americans.[31] Historian Albert Hart believed about terrorism, "The remedy most frequently invoked in the South, most widely applied and most strenuously defended, is to terrorize the Negro. Everybody knows that human life is less sacred in the South than in almost any other part of the civilized world."[32] Writing in the Political Science Quarterly, Albert McKinley shared his opinion about the culture of white supremacy:

The white man must rule but we want him to rule in the supremacy of decency and with the association of law and order which will command the respect not only of himself, but of the whole civilized world. Under the Negro and carpet bagger rule, the whites of the South were compelled either to leave their homes or to get control of the government. They chose the latter, since there was no place to which they could emigrate. There were two possible methods of assuming control: one was by force and shotguns, the other was to cheat the blacks.[33]

Private citizens shaped southern culture by creating a type of nationalism, uniting all whites at every social level, on issues mostly based on race.[34]

Historian Stuart Towns dubiously expressed his thoughts on Southern culture:

> Above all shaping the South, the Southern audience and the Southern speaker, there is the traditional memory of the South which has configured the way Southerners have lived for generations, regardless of whether it was "truth" or not: the moonlight and magnolias, mint juleps on the veranda, and Scarlet O'Hara of Gone with the Wind fame; the days of slavery and oppressions for a quarter of the population; the almost cultic worship and reverence of the Old South, the Confederacy, and the Lost Cause; the unpleasant memories of Reconstruction and the bitter and harsh Jim Crow laws of segregation days; the last stand to white supremacy and the difficult battles of the civil rights era; the sudden prosperity and the knowledge of being in the national spotlight—in a positive sense for a change. All this cultural memory, and more, is the South.[35]

Private citizens who upheld white supremacy exercised a deep rooted facet of southern culture. Writing in the American Journal of Sociology, George Howard provided suggestions to combat poor race relations in the region: "The solution will come through education, but it will come through the education of the white race. The white people of the South hold the point of vantage, and they must bear the responsibility. They should be wise leaders in the task of race-adjustment. That they have failed in the function of wise leadership is due to their retarded culture."[36]

Racism usually has more to do with an innate prejudicial feeling than with a system of domination.[37] Writing in The American Journal of Sociology W.F. Willcox asked, "Is race friction between whites and blacks in the United States likely to increase indefinitely or is it likely to reach a maximum after which its growth will slacken or stop?"[38] Similarly, writing in the Annals of the American Academy of Political and Social Science, W. D. Weatherford said, "The most difficult task is an attempt to understand the feelings that lie behind human beings who are brought into close juxtaposition. This is all the more difficult when the peoples brought into such relationship are different racial types."[39] Further, Professor Maurice Charland added his opinion about the South:

> As a means of making real our vision of a Southern Republic, we must first revitalize our largely Anglo-Celtic culture. Without a strong cultural base, political independence will be difficult to attain. But to strengthen Southern culture, we must overcome the mis-education of our people by undertaking a campaign to properly educate them about the history of the South in particular and America in general. To re-create Southern society, we should encourage the growth of largely self-sufficient communities among our people. We can develop healthy local communities and institutions by "abjuring the realm:" seceding from the mindless materialism and vulgarity of contemporary

American society. To stimulate the economic vitality of our people, we must become producers and not just consumers. By establishing "Buy Southern" programs and by forming trade guilds or associations, we can begin to wean ourselves from economic dependency. By encouraging the use of private sources of finance, such as cooperative loans instead of the Empire's banks, we can begin to break our financial dependency. Once we have planted the seeds of cultural, social, and economic renewal, then should we begin to look to the South's political renewal. Political independence will come only when we have convinced the Southern people that they are indeed a nation in the organic, historical, and Biblical sense of the word, namely, that they are a distinct people with a language, mores, and folkways that separate them from the rest of the world.[40]

Also, in preserving white supremacy, the younger generation of boys imitated the older generation of men. For example, they would carry rifles for self-defense and resist violently to alleged insults by black Americans.[41] Psychology Professors Richard Nisbett and Dov Cohen explained in their view the Southern culture of honor:

To maintain credible power of deterrence, the individual must project a stance of willingness to commit mayhem and to risk wounds or death for himself. Thus he must constantly be on guard against affronts that could be construed by others as disrespect. When someone allows himself to be insulted, he risks giving the impression that he lacks the strength to protect what is his. Thus the individual must respond with violence or the threat of violence to any affront.[42]

Lynching and politics have always been interrelated, wherein violence was rooted in Southern culture.[43] Author historian David Fischer also noted Southern natives' behavior:

In the absence of any strong sense of order as unity, hierarchy, or social peace, back settlers shared an idea of order as a system of retributive justice. The prevailing principle was lextalionis, the rule of retaliation. It held that a good man must seek to do right in the world, but when wrong was done to him, he must punish the wrongdoer himself by an act of retribution that restored order and justice in the world.[44]

Black Americans persistently sought the national government's attention to the severity of violence inflicted upon them. For proof that this was happening to them, anti-lynching activists collected as much evidence possible.[45] In addition, inasmuch as governors sought national assistance to prevent lynching, Representative Theodore Burton of Ohio opined to allow the states to handle its judicial affairs:

The tendency to centralization has no doubt been greatly promoted by the failures of states and minor communities to prove equal to the occasions which arise. It is especially true that if the states seek to have the federal government do something for which each state might do for itself, this will notably strengthen the power of the federal government. Under an ideal condition each city and state should not only be actuated by a desire to accomplish the greatest possible good for the whole people, but should be marked as well by efficiency in attaining great results. If states fall below this ideal condition it is not the fault of the central government, but of the citizens of each state.[46]

Contrary to traditional opinion, congressional investigative powers are broad[47] enough power to serve as a catalysts in dire situations. Assistant Attorney General Guy Goff argued that the policing powers between the two levels of government are mutual:

> Wherever the Constitution has delegated to Congress certain rights and duties, which Congress is permitted to bound to enforce and to carry out, the extent to which Congress may go in thus enforcing rights or fulfilling duties within the limitations prescribed by the Constitution is sufficiently great to permit of the exercise of a Federal police power, and the exercise of this Federal police power is neither repugnant to nor superior to the police power of the State. Each is concurrent with the other.[48]

While the states' rights debate is the oldest constitutional debate,[49] Twentieth century Attorney General Harry Daugherty furnished his own analysis about the federal-civil rights debate: "To my mind there can be no doubt that negativity on the part of the State may be, as well as any act of a positive nature by such State, a denial of the equal protection of the laws and thus be within the prohibition of the Fourteenth Amendment so as to give Congress power to act with reference to it."[50]

When cases are heard before federal judges, their primary responsibility involves interpreting the text of the Constitution.[51] During this time, very few if any lynching incidents reached the Supreme Court. The Supreme Court also believed in states' rights to remedy lynching. NAACP board member Herbert Stockton expressed his views about the federal judiciary's role:

> You know and I know, everybody, even the individual members of the Supreme Court know that the victims of lynching mobs do not get the equal protection of the State's law, that State and County officials do not try to prevent this crime as they try to prevent other crimes. This is susceptible of overwhelming convincing demonstration in graphic detail, so that this record can be brought before the Supreme Court when it passes on the constitutionality of the law. The bill is in accord with the fundamental purpose of this amendment for the Federal Government to take action to ensure the Negroes

particularly, equal protection; their plight was the cause of the amendment's being adopted, their plight now is the occasion of this legislation.[52]

As a result of the democratic solidarity in the Senate, bills for civil rights were difficult to become legislation. Southern Democrats stood together in every effort to oppose civil rights for black Americans. Despite their unity, federal intervention was still necessary to govern unruly private citizens. Since to prevent lynching required the assistance of the national government, anti-lynching activists refused to accept the argument that it was a problem that the states should handle. Historical evidence reveals that racism was profoundly embedded in Southern culture. Given these points, it is impossible to believe that racism did not motivate the filibuster. Representative Champ Clark of Missouri asked:

> Is filibustering ever justifiable? The argument against cloture in the Senate is that there should be some place in our system of government where can be discussed fully which is absolutely true; but even a good thing can be over-done, and unquestionable it is sometimes overdone in the Senate. When a filibuster against a particular measure is carried to such an extreme as to defeat measures absolutely necessary for the public welfare, it becomes not only a farce, but a nuisance, and should be abated.[53]

NOTES

1. Robert Miles and Malcolm Brown, *Racism*, 2nd ed. (London: Routledge, 2003), 171.

2. Susan E. Babbitt and Sue Campbell, eds., *Racism and Philosophy* (Ithaca, NY: Cornell University Press, 1999), 80.

3. Ibid., 91.

4. Kenneth J. Neubeck and Noel A. Cazenave, *Welfare Racism: Playing the Race Card against America's Poor* (New York: Routledge, 2001), 242.

5. Michael J. Klarman, *From Jim Crow to Civil Rights: The Supreme Court and the Struggle for Racial Equality* (New York: Oxford University Press, 2004), 446.

6. James Waller, *Face to Face: The Changing State of Racism across America* (New York: Insight Books, 1998), 220.

7. Ibid., 226.

8. Ibid., 227.

9. Joe R. Feagin and Melvin P. Sikes, *Living with Racism: The Black Middle-Class Experience* (Boston: Beacon Press, 1994), 321.

10. Ibid., 240.

11. Ibid., 245.

12. C. James Trotman., *Frederick Douglass: a Biography (Greenwood Biographies)* (Santa Barbara, CA: Greenwood, 2011), 135.

13. Darlene Clark Hine, William C. Hine, and Stanley Harold, *The African-American Odyssey*, 5th ed. (Upper Saddle River, NJ: Pearson, 2011), 35.

14. John Milton Cooper Jr., *Woodrow Wilson: a Biography* (New York: Vintage, 2011), 411.

15. Ibid., 11.

16. Woodrow Wilson, "The States and the Federal Government," *The North American Review* 187 (1908): 684.

17. Ida B. Wells-Barnett, *Southern Horrors: Lynch Law in All Its Phases* (ReadHowYou-Want, 2009), 27.

18. John W. Blassingame and John R. McKivigan, *The Frederick Douglass Papers: Series One; Speeches, Debates, and Interviews; Vol.5, 1881-1895* (New Haven, CT: Yale University Press, 1992), 93.

19. Philip A. Klinkner and Rogers M. Smith, *The Unsteady March: the Rise and Decline of Racial Equality in America* (Chicago, IL: University of Chicago Press, 2002), 73.

20. Walter L. Fleming, *Documentary History of Reconstruction: Political, Military, Social, Religious, Educational and Industrial 1865 to the Present Time Vol.2* (Whitefish, MT: Kessinger Publishing, LLC, 2006), 229–30.

21. Alan D. DeSantis, "Selling the American Dream to Black Southerners: The Chicago Defender and the Great Migration of 1915–1919," *Western Journal of Communications* 62 (1998): 477–79.

22. Jacob U. Gordon, *Black Leadership for Social Change* (Westport, CT: Praeger, 2000), 108.

23. Phillip Foner and Robert James Branham, *Lift Every Voice: African American Oratory, 1787–1900* (Tuscaloosa, AL: University of Alabama Press, 1998), 786.

24. Godfrey Benson and Baron Charnwood, *Theodore Roosevelt* (University of Michigan: Atlantic Monthly Press, 1913), 99.

25. Theodore Roosevelt, "International Peace," *The Advocate of Peace (1894–1920)* 72 (1910): 146.

26. Chicago Commission on Race Relations, *The Negro in Chicago: a Study of Race Relations and a Race Riot* (Chicago, IL: Univ. Chicago Press, 1923), xiii.

27. Vron Ware, *Beyond the Pale: White Women, Racism and History* (London: Verso, 1992), 175.

28. Robin D. G. Kelley and Earl Lewis, eds., *To Make Our World Anew: Volume I: a History of African Americans to 1880* (New York: Oxford University Press, 2005), 346.

29. Ida B. Wells-Barnett, *Ida B. Wells on Lynching* (Amherst, NY: Humanity Books, 2002), 50.

30. Luther Z. Rosser, "The Illegal Enforcement of Criminal Law," *The Virginia Law Register* 7 (1921): 584.

31. Gunnar Myrdal, *An American Dilemma: the Negro Problem and Modern Democracy* (New Brunswick, NJ: Transaction Publishers, 1996), 478.

32. Albert Bushnell Hart, "The Outcome of the Southern Race Question," *The North American Review* 188 (1908): 55.

33. Albert E. McKinley, "Two New Southern Constitutions," *Political Science Quarterly* 18 (1903): 486.

34. Numan V. Bartley, ed., *The Evolution of Southern Culture* (Athens: University of Georgia Press, 1988), xii.

35. W. Stuart Towns, Oratory and Rhetoric in the Nineteenth Century South: A Rhetoric of Defense (Westport: Praeger, 2000): 5.

36. George Elliott Howard, "The Social Cost of Southern Race Prejudice," *American Journal of Sociology* 22 (1917): 577.

37. bell hooks, *Killing Rage: Ending Racism (Owl Book)*, Reprint ed. (New York: Holt Paperbacks, 1996), 108.

38. W. F. Willcox, "Is Race Friction between Blacks and Whites in the United States Growing and Inevitable," *American Journal of Sociology* 13 (1908): 820.

39. W. D. Weatherford, "Race Relationship in the South," *Annals of the American Academy of Political and Social Science* 49 (1913): 164.

40. Maurice Charland, "Constitutive Rhetoric: The Case of the Peuple Quebecois," *Quarterly Journal of Speech* 73 (1987): 139.

41. Gary M. Ciuba, *Desire, Violence, and Divinity in Modern Southern Fiction: Katherine Anne Porter, Flannery O'connor, Cormac Mccarthy, Walker Percy (Southern Literary Studies)*, Reprint ed. (Baton Rouge, LA: Louisiana State University Press, 2011), 18.

42. Richard E. Nisbett and Dov Cohen, *Culture of Honor: The Psychology of Violence in the South* (Boulder, CO: Westview Press, 1996), xv.

43. Gilles Vandal, *Rethinking Southern Violence: Homicides in Post-Civil War Louisiana, 1866–1884*, The History of Crime and Criminal Justice Series (Columbus: Ohio State University Press, 2000), 14.

44. Fischer, D. H., *Albion's Seed: Four British folkways in America* (New York: Oxford University Press, 1989), 765.

45. Gilles Vandal, *Rethinking Southern Violence: Homicides in Post-Civil War Louisiana, 1866–1884*, 183.

46. Theodore E. Burton, "Development of the Federal Government," *Annals of the American Academy of Political and Social Science* 32 (1908): 215.

47. Martin O. James, *Congressional Oversight* (New York: Nova Science, 2002), 32.

48. *Constitutionality of a Federal Antilynching Bill,* pt. 2, 38-39.

49. Sotirios A. Barber, *The Fallacies of States ' Rights* (Cambridge, MA: Harvard University Press, 2013), 1.

50. *Constitutionality of a Federal Antilynching Bill,* pt. 3, 57.

51. Antonin Scalia, *A Matter of Interpretation: Federal Courts and the Law (University Center for Human Values)*, ed. Amy Gutmann (Princeton, NJ: Princeton University Press, 1998), 13.

52. Herbert Stockton to William E. Borah, June 5, 1922, Storey Papers, Box 21, 2–3.

53. Champ Clark, "Cloture," *The North American Review* 201 (1915): 519.

Chapter Four

White Supremacy,
the Unwritten Law of the Land

"To hell with the law" was the boldness attitude of private citizens. Historian Howard Smead explained how white supremacy reigned as the law of the twentieth century, "Since Reconstruction, blacks have been executed at the whim of white mobs in defiance of the law because white supremacy took precedence over the law. In fact, white supremacy was the unwritten law of the land and created a code of justice for blacks under the rubric of Southern justice."[1] According to Professor J. Douglas Smith, white supremacy can be defined as "[a] disease that distorted and crippled the personalities of all southerners, black and white."[2] Southern politics deviated from the national norm by establishing a social hierarchy based solely on racism.[3] These types of racial strains escalated into violence when black Americans challenged the status quo.[4] Southern politics preferred a national government that did not interfere in its local affairs.[5] Without adherence for even state law against lynching, private citizens who formed as lynch mobs resembled anarchism.[6] The *San Francisco Call* newspaper reported lynching as a form of anarchy:

> The President also embraces the opportunity to express his own views in reference to lynching and mob violence as one form of anarchy, and that anarchy a forerunner of tyranny. The President vigorously urges that the penalty for crimes that induce a resort to lynching shall be applied swiftly and surely, but by due process of the courts, so that it may be deemed strictly that the law is adequate to deal with crime by freeing it from every vestige of technicality and delay.[7]

Attorney General A. A. Carmichael, Birmingham, Alabama judge Robert J. Wheeler, and the chair of a joint veterans' committee aggressively explained that the state could solve its own problems without the benefit of outside help. State legislatures demanded that the national government not investigate into the state judiciary. Although no action followed, state lawmakers relied on the state law enforcement to prevent private citizens from lynching.[8] When Southerners preferred federal absence, the National Negro Council dissented and compared the national government's absence to Pontius Pilate's washing of his hands.[9] The *Pittsburg Courier* reported the national inattention to lynching:

> Not a single person has been arrested or indicted for this crime, and it now begins to look as if none will be. How is it that men who could catch the most elusive criminals in the world are unable to track down a few back country Georgia murderers? It all seems very strange, and we suggest that J. Edgar Hoover cancel some of his scheduled speeches on suppressing crime and give his undivided attention to solving this one.[10]

When the Federal Elections Bill of 1890 was also filibustered for the same reasons of states' rights, some expressed opinions in Republican newspapers from all over the United States.[11] *Chicago Inter-Ocean*, January 10, 1889: "Congress can now provide the machinery for the election of members of the House, irrespective of State law." *Philadelphia Press*, December 4, 1889: "This will accomplish better results than the law taking the operation of Congressional elections under Federal control." *Baltimore American*, December 4, 1889: "President Harrison frankly recommends that Congress assume the supervision of the election of its own members, so that in National affairs, at least, the colored people can secure the representation and recognition guaranteed them by the Constitution." *Boston Journal*, March 17, 1890: "It is an honest and elaborate effort to accomplish a much-desired end." *Toledo Blade*, June 28, 1890: "Federal elections should be divided, in all the States, from any and all State elections. They should be entirely distinct and separate and held under the authority and control of Federal officers." *New York Press*, August 26, 1890: "This bill is in an entirely different Constitutional direction, for it extends the right of suffrage from theory to practice, and popularizes the national government." *Philadelphia Press*, January 27, 1891: "There was never a better test of genuine Republicanism than the elections bill." *Indianapolis Journal*, in January, 1891: All honor to those who stood by the principles of the party and in favor of honest elections." *Seattle Post-Intelligencer*, July 18, 1892: "As a proper measure to protect and purify the ballot-box it is to be regretted that the Senate of the 51st Congress failed to pass it." *Brooklyn Times*, July 25, 1892: "The Constitution of the United States does explicitly authorize Congress to provide that no local triumph of fraudulent methods shall work injury or injustice in Federal elections to the citizens of other States. Surely the time has come to give effect to this Constitutional provision." *Philadelphia Press*, July 30, 1892:

"The Republican party believes that every man in the Republic entitled to a vote should be allowed to exercise the right of suffrage. And it will stand on that preposition gladly for all time." *New York Age*, August 13, 1892: "A just Federal elections law is one of the things as certain to come as the eventual triumph of the Afro-American over all the powers of antagonism in the Republic." *New Haven Palladium*, August, 1892: "The party is committed to the theory that free and honest elections can be best secured through Federal legislation and the protection of the Federal government."[12]

The Democrats stood firm in opposition to the Federal Elections Bill that would have helped black Americans' secure their voting rights. Such vehemence against federal protection were found at the 1892 Democratic platform: "Such a policy, if sanctioned by law, would mean the dominance of a self-perpetuating oligarchy of office-holders, and the party first entrusted with its machinery could be dislodged from power only by an appeal to the reserved rights of the people to resist oppression which is inherent in all self-governing communities." Grover Cleveland too opposed federal intervention. Upon accepting his New York governorship nomination, he exclaimed, "The interference of officials of any degree, whether State or Federal, for the purpose of thwarting or controlling the popular wish should not be tolerated."[13] Democratic Vice-Presidential Candidate, Mr. Adlai Stevenson denounced the Federal Elections Bill robustly, "To the people of the Southern States it is one of transcendent importance-shall they still have peace and the protection of the law, or shall the horrors with which they are menaced find their counterpart only in those of the darkest hours of the reconstruction period?"[14]

Though a number of opponents resisted, Whitelaw Reid, editor of the *New York Tribune* did favor the bill by stating, "No other measure proposed at the present session of Congress is of greater or more far-reaching importance than this. The duty of Congress to secure honest elections is one which Republican Representatives cannot afford to neglect, for the result in Congressional elections in many Northern States may depend upon their action."[15]

Historian Janet Hudson believed what to be the common denominator in Southern culture, "The shared commitment to white supremacy united whites but only to the end of maintaining white control."[16] Editor Deidre Mullane explained how black Americans' service in the military should equate their constitutional right for civil rights:

> The black man cannot protect a country, if the country doesn't protect him and if tomorrow, a war should arise, I would not raise a musket to defend a country where my manhood is denied. The fashionable way in Georgia when hard work is to be done, is for the white man to sit at this ease, while the black man does the work; but, sir, I will say this much to the colored men of Georgia,

never lift a finger nor raise a hand in defense of Georgia, unless Georgia
acknowledges that you are men, and invests you with the rights pertaining to
manhood. [17]

Historian George Frederickson argued against white supremacy, "The
one thing that held the post-Reconstruction Democratic Party together was a
commitment to maintaining white supremacy." [18] NAACP President Moorfield Storey also complained of private citizens going unpunished, "Thirty
years' experience has demonstrated the fact that the Southern states will not
perform their duty. Not only are they not disposed to stop lynching, but they
approve of it. They say they do not. They profess to be shocked by the
atrocities, but they do not lift their fingers to stop them." [19] *The Crisis*, an
official publication of the NAACP condemned the government similarly, "It
is perfectly true that most white Southerners are not lynchers, but it is just as
true that most of them will not consent to the one step which will stop
lynching, punishment of lynchers." [20]

Twentieth century sociologist Howard Odum addressed what he called
the Negro problem as possibly an explanation as to why black Americans'
presence was so problematic in the South:

> There is a decided tendency on the part of both individuals and communities to
> reduce any and all problems that arise because of the presence of the Negroes
> in the United States to one commonly accepted composite "The Negro Prob-
> lem." Most of the local problems of the Negro are local in name only. A
> fundamental step of one community is of basic importance to a whole group of
> communities, which find it necessary to deal with the same question. [21]

Historian William Starr Myers also explained that the two race co-exist-
ing stimulated violent confrontations, "The Negroes must be taught pride and
solidarity, and the two races must arrive at some basis of common occupancy
of their respective territories, which shall be mutually satisfactory, even if
not wholly free from friction." [22] Clergyman John R. Straton presented solv-
able questions concerning the poorly structured race relations:

> Will education solve the race problem? That is, will it bring about such an
> advance on the part of the Negro as will adapt him fully to his environments
> and make him a worthy integer in our national life, if he is allowed fully to
> enter that life, by the breaking down of the race prejudice and antipathy against
> him? If education will not accomplish the desired advance, what are the causes
> which prevent such a result? There are reasons for fearing that the hope for the
> solution of the race problem through education is based upon inadequate
> grounds. One of the most vital factors in the problem is the Negro's tendency
> to immorality and crime. This tendency in the colored race is of fundamental
> importance in any consideration of the problem because, if it continues, it
> means, instead of the hoped for growth, permanent decay and degeneracy in

every particular, it is safe to say that practically the entire Negro race was illiterate. The second is that, previous to the war, the Negro was not more criminal than other men.[23]

Writing in The North American Review, Joseph Proffit agreed with Straton that the lynching remedy is not to be found in legislation but rather in education:

> It is not to be found in placing laws upon our statute books which will never be enforced. Our laws from time immemorial have provided against murder. Lynching is murder. Legislation could only punish; it could never prevent. The true remedy is in education-an education exerting a two-fold influence. All things come by education or the want of it. Lynching is the result of long years of schooling in the practice. If we would see a cessation of mob rule we must unteach those who engage in it.[24]

Governor William Jelks of Alabama furnished his opinion on Southern race relations:

> It would be far better if the two races could be separated. The tension between them in most of the Southern States has been very great, though less serious in Alabama than in other Southern States, and less serious now than in the early part or middle of last year. Aside from this view, and for other reasons which might be named that prompt me to wish a separation, the Negro could grow in a home of his own. At least he would have an opportunity to do so, and, less pessimistic than others, I believe that he might achieve a fair government.[25]

Writing in The Advocate of Peace, George Cutter identified the roots of racism in Southern culture:

> Race prejudice is largely responsible for the dreadful lynchings of Negroes in the South. Since they were no better than cattle, why might not the whites hang, burn, mutilate, and murder them, when suspected of offenses, without appealing to the proper officers or waiting for the intervention of courts? There seemed to be some slight excuse for such summary vengeance when the suspected men were charged with criminal assault. But the law provided for all such cases, and before any jury in a hysterical and murderous community the chance of an acquittal of a guilty man was infinitesimally small. Such outrages used to be confined to the South, but the recent brutal and barbarous treatment of a Negro at Coatesville, Pennsylvania, shows that the malign spirit is spreading to the North. It shows, furthermore, an utter lack of justice and humanity; shows how thin a veneer covers our boasted civilization; shows what a hollow pretense is much of our Christianity as a practical force in public affairs, and how easily we can relapse from our lofty ideals of equality and fraternity to the degrading passions and demoralizing practices of a frenzied mob.[26]

Sociologist Monroe Work professed the underlying problems to race relations, "One of the most significant and hopeful signs for the satisfactory solution of the race problem in the South is the attitude that is being taken toward Negro crime."[27] Philosopher Josiah Royce also posed penetrating questions to the race relations matter:

> How can the white man and the Negro, once forced, as they are in our South, to live side by side, best learn to live with a minimum of friction, with a maximum of cooperation? I have long learned from my Southern friends that this end can only be attained by a firm, and by a very constant and explicit insistence upon keeping the Negro in his proper place, as a social inferior-who, then, as an inferior, should, of course, be treated humanely, but who must first be clearly and unmistakably taught where he belongs. [28]

The struggle for civil rights was ongoing in the twentieth century. The pursuit was more difficult especially when white supremacy was reestablished in the post-Reconstruction era.[29] The era of Reconstruction caused black Americans to seek the national government rather than the states for legal protection and to ensure their rights. Black Americans undoubtedly supported national control and expanding national power.[30] According to former University of Iowa Law Professor Emlin McClain, lynched victims were left vulnerable, "The law of the land affords a remedy to the individual for injuries done or threatened to him by other individuals. The individual harmed is left to rely on the remedies which the law of his state provides."[31] However, despite the dishonorable attitude toward black Americans, Attorney General Charles Bonaparte spoke positive of the lynched victims, "I believe that very few innocent men are lynched, and, of those who had not committed the past offense for which they suffer, a still smaller proportion are decent members of society."[32] Historian Leon Litwack illustrated those types of decent members in society:

> The men and women who tortured, dismembered, and murdered in this fashion understood perfectly well what they were doing and thought of themselves as perfectly normal human beings. Few had any ethical qualms about their actions. What is most disturbing about these scenes is the discovery that the perpetrators of the crimes were ordinary people, not so different from ourselves; they were family men and women, good churchgoing folk. [33]

Attorney General Daugherty encouraged private citizens to adhere to state law against lynching, "Let it be hoped that we shall all calm down, and come to recognize that in a country of law, of our own law, we must learn to respect the law."[34] NAACP Secretary Walter White mentioned how much lynching resonated even in the home, "Society had degenerated to a point where an uncomfortably large percentage of Americans can read in their newspapers of the slow roasting alive of a human being in Mississippi and turn, promptly and with little thought, to the comic strip or sporting page."[35] In cases of rape, the NAACP's Director of Publicity Herbert J. Seligmann suggested, "The tree is a monument to the spirit of manhood of this community who will not tolerate crimes against their women folks."[36] Along the same lines, writing in Fratenity, Celestine Edwards suggested that alleging rape brought about the mob, but was not always the case as to what happened:

> Not every white woman who yells rape has been raped against her will and not every black man lynched is charged with rape. Whatever may be the facts of the case, they should be ascertained and punished by the legal authorities and not by an irresponsible mob of the best citizens. And no guilty man, be the rapist or mobocrat, ought to escape punishment.[37]

Black Americans' social and economic conditions were often unrelated to black criminality.[38] Writing in The Political Science Review, Gilbert Stephenson noted how black Americans were likely suspects of criminality, "The present vagrancy laws in most of the Southern States were aimed directly at the Negroes because of their indolence and thriftlessness."[39] Moreover, historian W.E.B DuBois observed black criminality in the South: The political status of the Negro in the South is closely connected with the question of Negro crime. There can be no doubt that crime among Negroes has greatly increased in the last twenty years and that there has appeared in the slums of great cities a distinct criminal class among the blacks.[40]

Conclusively, the Senate filibuster seemingly normalized white supremacy in the twentieth century and soon became overbearing for black Americans. Efforts to continue to employ legal tactics to prevent lynching began to wane. Now, ideas about personally retaliating against private citizens began to surface. For example, historian Herbert Shapiro said, "If they burn your houses, burn theirs. If they kill your wives and children, kill theirs. Pursue them relentlessly. Meet force with force, everywhere it is offered. If they demand blood, exchange with them until they are satiated. By a vigorous adherence to this course, the shedding of human blood by white men will soon become a thing of the past."[41]

NOTES

1. Howard Smead, *Blood Justice: The Lynching of Mack Charles Parker* (New York: Oxford University Press, 1988), x.

2. J. Douglas Smith, *Managing White Supremacy: Race, Politics, and Citizenship in Jim Crow Virginia* (Chapel Hill, NC: University of North Carolina Press, 2002), 289.

3. Nicol C. Rae, *Southern Democrats* (New York: Oxford University Press, 1994), 3.

4. Glenn Feldman, *Politics, Society, and the Klan in Alabama, 1915-1949* (Tuscaloosa, AL: University of Alabama Press, 1999), 12.

5. Byron E. Shafer and Richard Johnston, *The End of Southern Exceptionalism: Class, Race, and Partisan Change in the Postwar South* (Cambridge, MA: Harvard University Press, 2006), 3.

6. H.M. Daugherty, "Respect for Law," *American Bar Association Journal* 7 (1921), 505.

7. "President Denounces Lynching," *San Francisco Call*, August 10, 1903.

8. Ibid., 307.

9. Ibid., 313.

10. *Pittsburgh Courier*, October 5, 1946.

11. Democratic National Committee, *The Campaign Text Book of the Democratic Party for the Presidential Election of 1892 (Classic Reprint)* (London: Forgotten Books, 2012), 136.

12. Ibid., 139–40.

13. Ibid., 142.

14. Ibid., 144.

15. Ibid., 133.

16. Janet G. Hudson, *Entangled by White Supremacy: Reform in World War I-Era South Carolina* (Lexington, KY: University Press of Kentucky, 2009), 313.

17. Deirdre Mullane, *Crossing the Danger Water: Three Hundred Years of African-American Writing* (New York: Random House, 1993), 316.

18. George M. Fredrickson, *White Supremacy: A Comparative Study in American and South African History* (New York: Oxford University Press, 1981), 278.

19. Moorfield Storey to William Edgar Borah, February 14, 1922, Borah Papers, Box 106.

20. *Crisis*, January 1920, 110.

21. Howard W. Odum, "Some Studies in the Negro Problems of the Southern States," *The Journal of Race Development* 6 (1915): 185.

22. William Starr Myers, "Some Present-Day Views of the Southern Race Problem," *The Sewanee Review* 21 (1913): 347.

23. John Roach Straton, "Will Education Solve the Race Problem?" *The North American Review* 170 (1900): 785.

24. Joseph Edwin Proffit, "Lynching: Its Cause and Cure," *The Yale Law Journal* 7 (1898): 266.

25. William Dorsey Jelks, "The Acuteness of the Negro Question: A Suggested Remedy," *The North American Review* 184 (1907): 389.

26. George W. Cutter, "Race Prejudice," *The Advocate of Peace (1894-1920)* 73 (1911): 234.

27. Monroe N. Work, "Negro Criminality in the South," *Annals of the American Academy of Political and Social Science* 49 (1913): 80.

28. Josiah Royce, "Race Questions and Prejudices," *International Journal of Ethics* 16 (1906): 270.

29. Bryan M. Jack, *The St. Louis African American Community and the Exodusters* (Columbia: University of Missouri, 2008), 158.

30. Benjamin Quarles, *The Negro in the Making of America*, 3rd ed. (New York: Touchstone, 1996), 177.

31. Emlin McClain, "Constitutional Guarantees of Fundamental Rights" in *Modern American Law: A Systematic and Comprehensive Commentary on the Fundamental Principles of American Law and Procedure, Accompanied by Leading Illustrative Cases and Legal Forms with a Revised Edition of Blackstone's Commentaries,* ed. Eugene Allen Gilmore (Chicago, IL: Blackstone Institute, 1914), 42, 11–14, 94.

32. David, M. Kennedy, *Over Here: The First World War and American Society* (New York: Oxford University Press, 1980), 79.

33. Leon Litwack, "Hell Hounds" in *Without Sanctuary: Lynching Photography in America*, ed. James Allen (Santa Fe, NM: Twin Palms Press, 2000), 14.

34. "Lynchings in 1919," *The Literary Digest 64* (1920): 20.

35. Walter White, *Rope and Faggot: A Biography of Judge Lynch* (New York: Arno Press, 1969), 8.

36. Herbert J. Seligmann, "Protecting Southern Womanhood," *The Nation*, June 14, 1919.

37. Celestine Edwards, "Unity Our Aim," *Fratenity* 1 (1893): 1.

38. Khalil Gibran Muhammad, *The Condemnation of Blackness: Race, Crime, and the Making of Modern Urban America* (Cambridge: Harvard University Press, 2011), 35.

39. Gilbert Thomas Stephenson, "Racial Distinctions in Southern Law," *The American Political Science Review* 1 (1906): 59.

40. W. E. B. DuBois, "The Relation of the Negroes to the Whites in the South," *Annals of the American Academy of Political and Social Science* 18 (1901): 131.

41. Herbert Shapiro, *White Violence and the Black Response: From Reconstruction to Montgomery* (Amherst, MA: University of Massachusetts Press, 1988), 42.

Chapter Five

The Disappointment,
Stymied by Old Southern Politics

Historically, the national government has claimed its power of protecting black Americans' civil rights against violence when it claimed to protect newly freed slaves.[1] When the framers of the Fourteenth Amendment wrote that no state should "deprive any person of life, liberty, or property, without due process of law; nor deny to any person within its jurisdiction the equal protection of the laws," they were attempting to protect former slaves from discriminatory action by Confederate states. However, these clauses implied two significant themes. The first theme was that it was the duty of government to protect all persons in their civil rights, and the second theme was that all persons were equal before the law.[2]

NAACP board member Herbert Stockton pointed out the failures of the equal protection clause in the Fourteenth Amendment, "The victims of lynching mobs do not get the equal protection of the State's law, that State and County officials do not try to prevent this crime as they try to prevent other crimes."[3] Though the Fourteenth Amendment does apply to the states, the equal protection clause for black Americans then did not uphold its promise. "Its object is to preclude legislation by any State which shall deny due process and equal protection and Congress is empowered to pass all laws necessary to render such unconstitutional State legislation ineffectual."[4] Furthermore, in its clearest interpretive meaning, even the South had no regard for the Fourteenth Amendment's equal protection clause.[5] Writing *Lecture on the Fourteenth Article Amendment*, William Gutherie fervidly opposed for federal intervention and explained that lynching by private citizens was not to be addressed under the Fourteenth Amendment:

The federal courts cannot supervise or interfere with the internal affairs of a State unless some constitutional right has been invaded by state authority. The wrongful actions of individuals are not to be redressed under this amendment. They constitute private wrongs. The denial of a constitutional right must rest upon some state law or state authority for its excuse or perpetration if the Fourteenth Amendment is to furnish any remedy. Nor is the hardship or injustice of state laws necessarily an objection to their constitutional validity. The remedy for evils of that character is to be sought in the state legislature-not in the federal courts.[6]

A better understanding of the Fourteenth Amendment required that its application was best realized through the drafting of appropriate legislation rather than judicial interpretation.[7] Yet, reformer Albert Pillsbury still believed the Fourteenth Amendment was the principle foundation to drafting anti-lynching legislation:

It would seem that citizens of the United States, whatever may be said of other persons, are entitled to live in its peace, and to have preserved for the protection of their lives. If the United States can legislate directly for the preservation of its peace within the states, the pending bill appears to be within its powers. If the power and duty to preserve the peace of the United States within the states belongs solely to the states, the failure of the states to preserve it is a breach of duty toward the United States. In this view, the United States has power to deal with such a breach as an offense against itself, on the part of all individuals who contribute to it.[8]

Struggling for civil rights and protections from disorderly private citizens essentially characterizes African American History.[9] Going into the twentieth century, the quest for civil rights was problematic.[10] As a result of the inadequacy of state regulation of crime, a federal law prosecuting private citizens was necessary to remedy lynching. The failure of local law enforcement officials to break up mobs condoned lynching in a myriad of ways. Accordingly, and rightly so, Albert Pillsbury emphasized by not condemning lynching is in essence condoning it: "In view of direct interest of the U.S. in the lives of its citizens, who services for various purposes it has a right to command, it is monstrous to say that the U.S. has no power to protect them [black Americans] in their lives within the states if and so far as the states permit their murder by mobs failing to maintain an effective government of law and order."[11]

Grand juries did not indict and trial juries acquitted.[12] Ignoring or absolving rather than punishing and preventing violators of state laws against lynching actually encouraged private citizens.[13] Especially when governors sought national assistance, the national government carried responsibility for intervening.[14] Black Americans who challenged white supremacy were nonetheless killed. Private citizens used murder and violence to essentially bully black Americans.[15]

The NAACP agreed that private citizens killed black Americans at will, "As long as lynchers go unpunished, and officers of the law who protect them are immune from consequences which they ought to be made to suffer there will not be an end of such disgrace to the United States."[16] Representative Samuel Barrows of Massachusetts expressed his sentiments about inaction toward lynching, "Public sentiment in regard to the infliction of the death penalty in the United States shows itself both in the enactment of law and in the violation of law. In the violation of law it takes the form of lynching. Mob murder is not justified by statute but little has been done by statute to prevent it."[17] NAACP President Mooefield Storey rendered similar thoughts about no punishment for private citizens: "No attempt is made to punish the lynchers and that system has continued for years, so far as the colored people are concerned there is no republican government, and it should be possible for Congress to pass laws so as to ensure so large a section of our population their rights as citizens."[18]

Historian Philip Dray asked, "Is it possible for white America to really understand blacks' distrust of the legal system, their fears of racial profiling and the police without understanding how cheap a black life was for so long in our nation's history?"[19] Historian Mark Ellis also asked, "Is there not some way which we may assure the colored people that the government will take steps to bring justice to the perpetrators of this awful crime? I have no more sympathy for a man who is found guilty of a criminal assault on a woman, than I have for a lawless mob that will burn to death a human in a public square, rather than let the law take its course which would naturally mean death to the former."[20]

Legal scholar, Henry Black, stated his views on protecting black Americans: "The duty of protecting all its citizens with enjoyment of an equality of rights was originally assumed by the state and it still remains there. The only obligation resting with the United States is to see that the states do no deny the rights, no more. The power of the national government is limited to the enforcement of the guaranty."[21]

In federal judge Kenesaw Landis' view of federal intervention into state responsibility, he said, "The constant difficulty, which has confronted the Congress every time it has assumed to enter upon a similar field, is whether the Federal Government will enter upon the jurisdiction of a matter which States have already assumed the jurisdiction of, or whether it will wait until the State has concluded its efforts and then either cooperate or refuse to complicate the results by its interference."[22]

NAACP President Moorfield Storey also argued for the federal judiciary's actions:

The Supreme Court of the U.S. has held that the right to punish for the ordinary common law crime is within the exclusive jurisdiction of the States, and I think that any statute which undertakes to transfer that jurisdiction from the states to the federal courts, or which undertakes to make those crimes punishable under the federal statutes would not be upheld by the court. The law is that the rights and immunities which are created by the U.S. alone can be protected by federal legislation.[23]

Moreover, the Association of Southern Women for the Prevention of Lynching opposed states' rights to remedy lynching: "Two thirds of the executions of prisoners by mobs are due to one of two things, either cowardice of the sheriff or to a willingness for the mob to succeed, from the false conviction that a sheriff in fighting for them is not fighting for law but for some worthless prisoner. There is no prosecution. No strong voice ever condemns it."[24]

Finally, describing on federal oversight over civil rights, legal scholar Edward Corwin reasoned:

The Court in its early fear for the federal balance denied the Fourteenth Amendment practically all efficacy as a limitation upon State power, save in the interest of racial equality before the law. Subsequently, however, the Court found reason to abandon its early conservative position and take a greatly enlarged view of its supervisor power over State legislation, particularly of due process.[25]

In contrast, Assistant Attorney General John Crim explained his position on state remedy to lynching, "There is no federal statute punishing outrages by individuals upon colored people on accounts of the race. The only remedy is through the laws and the authorities of the particular State in which the outrages occur."[26] Editors Jessie Guzman and W. Hardin Hughes concluded similarly, "Any anti-lynching legislation brought before that body will be opposed by use of the filibuster. The main argument used against the bill is that it interferes with states' rights; and local governmental agencies can best cope with the situation."[27] So too, the *Houston Post* reported its position on states' rights:

The half-century old lynching problem is about to pass from the jurisdiction of state authority into the domain of federal action. Surely, in the light of a half century of lynching, in which the victims have numbered thousands, the failure of the states must be confessed. Federal action would be less hampered in dealing with the peculiar difficulties surrounding mob violence than the state processes have been.[28]

Justice William Brennan encouraged, "state courts to use their own constitutions and authority to protect individual rights."[29] Civil rights activists

Jessie Daniel Ames fervently held local officials responsible for private citizens who lynched, "If a mob does form and does attempt to act, suggest to the county officials that they file charges against the leaders for inciting to riot."[30] Additionally, Virginian John Tucker firmly believed in states' rights:

> While these Reconstruction amendments have increased the powers of the general government to some extent, and have abridged the powers of the States, and have given interpretation to the nature of the constitutional compact between them, yet that in all essentials, the system of our Constitutional Union, its structure and its fundamental principles have not been changed. It is a union of States, a double system of governments with justice, right and self-rule under the States, as the homes of the people.[31]

Also favoring states' rights, Representative Thomas Blanton of Texas said, "You can pass this law [anti-lynching] if you want to, but whenever we find it necessary we will lynch Negroes just the same."[32] On the grounds of Congressmen Blanton making this statement, old Southern politics with a racist's overtone was difficult to overcome. Elected Southern politicians had no trouble protecting white supremacy while in Congress.[33] In fact, protecting the racial status quo was paramount to their duties.[34] Democratic Senator Josiah Bailey affirmed his other Democratic colleagues of his position in the party when he boldly said, "The civilization in the South is going to be a white civilization; its government is going to be a white man's government."[35] As stated, Southern Democrats who had an old South mentality defended the South's racial traditions,[36] therefore, when contending to issues concerning race, congressmen audaciously made such statements as "the South won't stand for that."[37] Southern Democrats owned all of the political leadership in the South. These politicians, who were white Southern natives, took their prejudiced attitudes toward black Americans into Congress. Historically, the filibuster has been a legislative weapon to block the national government from taking action. Some congressmen remained in office until their maximum term limit and was able to successfully prevent the national government from intervening and acting on behalf of black Americans. Basically, they used their position in Congress to keep a pro-southern approach regarding racial matters.[38] It was no challenge for Southern Democrats to control racial issues because until the civil rights movement they filibustered civil rights bills to death. Prosecuting private citizens at the federal level could not be legislated because of Southern Democrats' racist's motivation to filibuster.[39]

The Dyer Anti-Lynching Bill called for more power from the national government where the state did not prosecute private citizens for lynching.[40] Congressmen Dyer assuredly proclaimed state inaction was reason enough for federal intervention:

It would seem to follow that when a citizen or other person is put to death by a lawless mob, in default of the protection which the State is bound to provide for all alike, there is a denial of equal protection by the State, in the sense of the equality clause, which Congress may prevent or punish by legislation applying to any individuals who participate in or contribute to it, directly or indirectly.[41]

In 1918 when Congressman Dyer introduced the anti-lynching bill it passed the House but failed in the Senate. Civil rights activists James Weldon Johnson remarked on the victory of the Dyer Bill passing in the House. After years of effort, he commented:

The passage of the Dyer Anti-Lynching Bill in the House of Representatives this afternoon by a vote of 230 to 119 is one of the most significant steps ever taken in the history of America. For the Negro it means that continual agitation has at least been answered and the appeal of the colored man to Congress for relief from mob violence has at least been granted. The reign of terrorism and anarchy must end is the message to lynchers that Congress has sent.[42]

However, when the bill was filibustered by Southern Democrats, historian W. E. B. DuBois eloquently expressed his discontent, "The manner of the defeat of the Dyer Anti-Lynching Bill emphasizes the fact that the machinery of the United States is antiquated to the point that millions of people may suffer injustice and death on account of it."[43]

Five years later the bill was reintroduced into Congress, but again defeated by Southern Democrats.[44] In 1930, Senators Edward Costigan of Colorado and Robert Wagner of New York introduced new anti-lynching bills in Congress. This particular bill, the Costigan-Wagner Anti-Lynching Bill, would punish law officers who failed to protect a person from the lynch mob.[45] The nearly 200 anti-lynching bills proposed in Congress was an attempt to get the national government to take an aggressive role in preventing lynchings by prosecuting private citizens. Essentially, had the bill passed, the federal courts would have punished private citizens and not the state courts.[46] Republicans stood by the fact that lynching violated black Americans' constitutional rights.[47] Moreover, after the many filibustered bills, the NAACP became discouraged and felt that legislation was an ineffective tool.[48] The NAACP felt that lynching was the single most important issue facing the country at the time.[49] In a number of ways, the organization was disappointed by the filibuster because they expected the national government to protect the rights of black Americans as it had done in the past.[50] In their view, each anti-lynching bill was an earnest attempt to provide black Americans with the legal rights they were entitled to.[51]

In final consideration, to understand the devastations wrought by race-based politics, Senate filibustering must be brought to attention of the public.

In evaluating the governmental system, the truth is, filibustering was a step backward in the quest for civil rights, where lynching perpetuated the status quo. To say the least, lynching was a form of bullying. Since there was no legislative victory, twentieth century bullying went uninterrupted and left anti-lynching activists thwarted. NAACP President Moorfield Storey fought for at least trying to enact a federal law against lynching by saying, "I recognize the legal difficulties, but I also recognize the dangers which confront us, and I had rather try and fail than throw up my hands and say that nothing can be done to relieve this country from the reputation for barbarity which is too richly deserved."[52] Even Representative Frederick Dallinger of Massachusetts agreed with Storey in that Congress should have put forth efforts to enact a federal law against lynching: "It has seemed to me a very doubtful question whether legislation by Congress against lynching in the States is constitutional, but I am very clearly of the opinion that it ought to be tried. At the most, the country will be no worse off if the experiment fails than it is now."[53]

If Southern Democrats held prejudiced views toward black Americans before they took office, then their same attitudes possibly motivated the filibuster. Criminalizing lynching on a federal level had to be based on a moral decision and not argued on the constitutionality of states' rights, where private citizens could get away with murder.

NOTES

1. "A Look at Federal Role in Civil Rights Cases," *Daily Herald (Arlington Heights, IL)*, August 19, 2013.

2. Robert P. Green, Jr., ed., *Equal Protection and the African American Constitutional Experience: A Documentary History* (Westport, CT: Greenwood Press, 2000), 1.

3. Herbert Stockton to William Edgar Borah, June 5, 1922, Storey Papers, Box 21, 2–3.

4. *Constitutional Limitations*, 8th ed., I, 602n.

5. Joseph B. James, *The Ratification of the Fourteenth Amendment* (Macon, GA: Mercer University Press, 1984), 9.

6. Guthrie, *Lecture on the Fourteenth Article of Amendment to the Constitution of the United States*, 102.

7. Robin West, *Progressive Constitutionalism: Reconstructing the Fourteenth Amendment* (Durham: Duke University Press Books, 1994), 6.

8. Albert Pillsbury to James Weldon Johnson, December 18, 1919.

9. Philip A. Goduti Jr., *Robert F. Kennedy and the Shaping of Civil Rights, 1960–1964* (Jefferson, NC: McFarland, 2012), 1.

10. United States. President's Committee on Civil Rights, *To Secure These Rights: The Report of the President's Committee on Civil Rights* (New York: Simon and Schuster, 1947), iii.

11. Albert Pillsbury to James Weldon Johnson, July 22, 1921, NAACP Records, Group I, Series C, Box 242.

12. Thomas I. Emerson and David Haber, *Political and Civil Rights in the United States* (Buffalo, NY: Dennis, 1952), 3.

13. C.F. Reavis's January conflict with Congressmen Edward Little. A13372 (Ansorge, January 25).

14. William Schwabe, Lois M. Davis, and Brian A. Jackson, *Challenges and Choices for Crime-Fighting Technology: Federal Support of State and Local Law Enforcement* (Santa Monica, CA: Rand, 2001), 13.

15. Brendan January, *Civil Rights* (Chicago: Heinemann, 2003), 14.

16. NAACP Anti-Lynching Papers, Reel 8/309.

17. Samuel J. Barrows, "Legislative Tendencies as to Capital Punishment," *Annals of the American Academy of Political and Social Science* 29 (1907): 178.

18. Moorfield Storey to William Paul Dillingham, Jan. 19, 1920 box C-75, NAACP-LC.

19. Philip Dray, *At the Hands of Persons Unknown: The Lynching of Black America* (New York: Random House, 2002), 11.

20. Mark Ellis, *Race, War, and Surveillance: African-Americans and the United States Government during World War II* (Bloomington, IN: Indiana University Press, 2001), 71.

21. Henry C. Black, *Handbook of American Constitutional Law*, 3d ed. (St. Paul, MN: West Publishing Company, 1910), 556.

22. Congressional Record, 65 Cong., 1 sess., 5152 (Lewis, July16, 1917).

23. William B. Hixson, Jr., *Moorfield Storey and the Abolitionist Tradition* (New York: Oxford University Press, 1972), 3–44.

24. Association of Southern Women for the Prevention of Lynching Papers (microfilm).

25. Edward Corwin, "The Supreme Court and the Fourteenth Amendment," in *American Constitutional History: Essays by Edward S. Corwin*, ed., Alpheus T. Mason and Gerald Garvey (New York, Evanston, and London: Harper and Row, 1964), 68–70.

26. John W. H. Crim to W. D. Johnson, June 8, 1922, responding to June 1, 1922 inquiry, Record Group 60, #158260–202.

27. Jessie P. Guzman and W. Hardin Hughes, "Lynching-Crime," *The Making of African American Identity* 3 (1917–1968): 9.

28. *Houston Post*, taken from *The New York Times*, March 9, 1919.

29. William J. Brennan Jr. "State Constitutions and the Protection of Individual Rights," *Harvard Law Review* 90 (1977): 489.

30. Jessie Daniel Ames Letter, Aug. 11, 1932, box 4, folder no. 31, JDA.

31. John R. Tucker, *The Constitution of the United States: A Critical Discussion of its Genesis, Development, and Interpretation*, ed., Henry St. George Tucker (2 vols., Chicago: Callaghan and Company, 1899), 846.

32. Sondra Kathryn Wilson, *In Search of Democracy: The NAACP Writings of James Weldon Johnson, Walter White, and Roy Wilkins (1920-1977)* (New York: Oxford University Press, 1999), 42.

33. Earl Black and Merle Black, *The Rise of Southern Republicans* (Cambridge, MA: Belknap Press, 2003), 3.

34. Ibid., 55.

35. Ibid., 32.

36. Ibid., 42.

37. Ibid., 43.

38. Ibid., 45.

39. Ibid., 52.

40. Nikki L. Brown and Barry M. Stentiford, eds. *The Jim Crow Encyclopedia.* The American Mosaic (Westport, CT: Greenwood, 2008), 256.

41. Congressional Record, 65 Cong., 2 Sess., 61 (May 7, 1918).

42. Megan Ming Francis, *Civil Rights and the Making of the Modern American State* (United Kingdom: Cambridge University Press, 2014), 98.

43. Ibid., 98,

44. Ibid., 197.

45. Ibid.

46. Ibid., 103.

47. Ibid.

48. Ibid., 99.

49. Ibid., 107.

50. Ibid., 100.

51. Horace Randall Williams and Ben Beard, *This Day in Civil Rights History* (Montgomery, AL: NewSouth Books, 2009), 87.

52. Moorfield Storey to George Wickersham, January 15, 1921, NAACP Records, Series I, Group C, Box 242.

53. Segregation and Antilynching, Part II: Antilynching, 22–23.

Appendix A

Profiles of the 51st–82nd Congress[1]

51ST CONGRESS (1889–1891)

332 Representatives
9 Delegates
152 Democrats
179 Republicans
Congressional Summary:
　　Congress enacted legislation: military pensions; naval expansion, Sherman Silver Purchase Act and Sherman Antitrust Act.
Speaker of the House: Thomas B. Reed (R–Maine)
Democratic Caucus Chairman: William S. Holman (D–Indiana)
Republican Conference Chairman: Thomas J. Henderson (R–Illinois)
Clerk of the House: Edward McPherson

52ND CONGRESS (1891–1893)

332 Representatives
4 Delegates
238 Democrats
86 Republicans
Congressional Summary:
　　Congress enacted legislation: Eight-hour workday for federal blue-collar workers and new safety requirements on railway companies, also this Congress renewed the Chinese Exclusion Act for 10 years.
Speaker of the House: Charles F. Crisp (D–Georgia)

Democratic Caucus Chairman: William S. Holman (D–Indiana)
Republican Conference Chairman: Thomas J. Henderson (R–Illinois)
Clerk of the House: James Kerr

53RD CONGRESS (1893–1895)

356 Representatives
4 Delegates
218 Democrats
124 Republicans
Congressional Summary:
 Southern Democrats repealed the Reconstruction-era Force Acts that required federal supervision of Southern elections.
Speaker of the House: Charles F. Crisp (D–Georgia)
Democratic Caucus Chairman: William S. Holman (D–Indiana)
Republican Conference Chairman: Thomas J. Henderson (R–Illinois)
Clerk of the House: James Kerr

54TH CONGRESS (1895–1897)

357 Representatives
4 Delegates
93 Democrats
254 Republicans
Congressional Summary:
 This Congress approved an arbitration commission over the Venezuela-British Guiana boundary dispute.
Speaker of the House: Thomas B. Reed (R–Maine)
Democratic Caucus Chairman: David B. Culberson (D–Texas)
Republican Conference Chairman: Charles H. Grosvenor (R–Ohio)
Clerk of the House: Alexander McDowell

55TH CONGRESS (1897–1899)

357 Representatives
3 Delegates
124 Democrats
206 Republicans
Congressional Summary:
 This Congress annexed Hawaii and enacted the Dingley Tariff.
Speaker of the House: Thomas B. Reed (R–Maine)
Democratic Caucus Chairman: James D. Richardson (D–Tennessee)

Republican Conference Chairman: Charles H. Grosvenor (R–Ohio)
Clerk of the House: Alexander McDowell

56TH CONGRESS (1899–1901)

357 Representatives
4 Delegates
161 Democrats
187 Republicans
Congressional Summary:

    This Congress formed civil governments in the Philippines, Puerto Rico, and Alaska. Congress also provided a civil government and nonvoting Delegate for Hawaii and extended U.S. citizenship to the people who lived on the island.

Speaker of the House: David B. Henderson (R–Iowa)
Majority Leader: Sereno E. Payne (R–New York)
Minority Leader: James D. Richardson (D–Tennessee)
Democratic Caucus Chairman: James Hay (D–Virginia)
Republican Conference Chairman: Joseph G. Cannon (R–Illinois)
Clerk of the House: Alexander McDowell

57TH CONGRESS (1901–1903)

357 Representatives
4 Delegates
151 Democrats
200 Republicans
Congressional Summary:

    This Congress authorized funds to build a canal in Panama linking the Pacific Ocean with the Caribbean Sea.

Speaker of the House: David B. Henderson (R–Iowa)
Majority Leader: Sereno E. Payne (R–New York)
Minority Leader: James D. Richardson (D–Tennessee)
Democratic Caucus Chairman: James Hay (D–Virginia)
Republican Conference Chairman: Joseph G. Cannon (R–Illinois)
Clerk of the House: Alexander McDowell

58TH CONGRESS (1903–1905)

386 Representatives
4 Delegates
176 Democrats

207 Republicans
Congressional Summary:
This Congress enabled the Forest Service to better protect lumber reserves.
Speaker of the House: Joseph G. Cannon (R–Illinois)
Majority Leader: Sereno E. Payne (R–New York)
Minority Leader: John Sharp Williams (D–Mississippi)
Democratic Caucus Chairman: James Hay (D–Virginia)
Republican Conference Chairman: William P. Hepburn (R–Iowa)
Clerk of the House: Alexander McDowell

59TH CONGRESS (1905–1907)

386 Representatives
5 Delegates
135 Democrats
251 Republicans
Congressional Summary:
This Congress enacted the Pure Food and Drug Act; established the Bureau of Immigration and Naturalization, passed legislation to limit contract laborers, and created new regulations for issuing U.S. passports.
Speaker of the House: Joseph G. Cannon (R–Illinois)
Majority Leader: Sereno E. Payne (R–New York)
Minority Leader: John Sharp Williams (D–Mississippi)
Democratic Caucus Chairman: Robert L. Henry (D–Texas)
Republican Conference Chairman: William P. Hepburn (R–Iowa)
Clerk of the House: Alexander McDowell

60TH CONGRESS (1907–1909)

391 Representatives
5 Delegates
167 Democrats
223 Republicans
Congressional Summary:
This Congress produced the Aldrich-Vreeland Emergency Currency Act and established a National Monetary Commission.
Speaker of the House: Joseph G. Cannon (R–Illinois)
Majority Leader: Sereno E. Payne (R–New York)
Minority Leader: James Beauchamp Clark (D–Missouri); John Sharp Williams (D–Mississippi)
Democratic Caucus Chairman: Henry D. Clayton (D–Alabama)

Republican Conference Chairman:William P. Hepburn (R–Iowa)
Clerk of the House: Alexander McDowell

61ST CONGRESS (1909–1911)

391 Representatives
4 Delegates
172 Democrats
219 Republicans
Congressional Summary:
   This Congress passed the 16th Amendment authorizing an income tax.
Speaker of the House: Joseph G. Cannon (R–Illinois)
Majority Leader: Sereno E. Payne (R–New York)
Minority Leader: James Beauchamp Clark (D–Missouri)
Democratic Caucus Chairman: Henry D. Clayton (D–Alabama)
Republican Conference Chairman: Frank D. Currier (R–New Hampshire)
Clerk of the House: Alexander McDowell

62ND CONGRESS (1911–1913)

394 Representatives
4 Delegates
230 Democrats
162 Republicans
Congressional Summary:
   This Congress sent the 17th Amendment for the direct election of Senators to the states. Other legislation included: a separate Labor Department, a Children's Bureau, and an eight-hour workday required for all federal contractors.
Speaker of the House: James Beauchamp Clark (D–Missouri)
Majority Leader: Oscar W. Underwood (D–Alabama)
Minority Leader: James R. Mann (R–Illinois)
Democratic Caucus Chairman: Albert S. Burleson (D–Texas)
Republican Conference Chairman: Frank D. Currier (R–New Hampshire)
Clerk of the House: South Trimble

63RD CONGRESS (1913–1915)

435 Representatives
2 Delegates
291 Democrats
134 Republicans

Speaker of the House: James Beauchamp Clark (D–Missouri)
Majority Leader: Oscar W. Underwood (D–Alabama)
Minority Leader: James R. Mann (R–Illinois)
Democratic Caucus Chairman: A. Mitchell Palmer (D–Pennsylvania)
Republican Conference Chairman: William S. Greene (R–Massachusetts)
Clerk of the House: South Trimble

64TH CONGRESS (1915–1917)

435 Representatives
2 Delegates
230 Democrats
196 Republicans
Congressional Summary:
   This Congress increased military preparedness and established a U.S. Shipping Board. Congress also granted full U.S. citizenship to Puerto Ricans.
Speaker of the House: James Beauchamp Clark (D–Missouri)
Majority Leader: Claude Kitchin (D–North Carolina)
Minority Leader: James R. Mann (R–Illinois)
Democratic Caucus Chairman: Edward W. Saunders (D–Virginia)
Republican Conference Chairman: William S. Greene (R–Massachusetts)
Clerk of the House: South Trimble

65TH CONGRESS (1917–1919)

435 Representatives
2 Delegates
214 Democrats
215 Republicans
Congressional Summary:
   This Congress declared war on Germany. Congress also sent to the states a constitutional amendment banning the production and sale of alcohol.
Speaker of the House: James Beauchamp Clark (D–Missouri)
Majority Leader: Claude Kitchin (D–North Carolina)
Minority Leader: James R. Mann (R–Illinois)
Democratic Caucus Chairman: Edward W. Saunders (D–Virginia)
Republican Conference Chairman: William S. Greene (R–Massachusetts)
Clerk of the House: South Trimble

66TH CONGRESS (1919–1921)

435 Representatives

2 Delegates
192 Democrats
240 Republicans
Congressional Summary:

This Congress approved the 18th Amendment banning the production, transportation, and sale of alcohol. Congress implemented Prohibition with passage of the Volstead Act. Congress also sent the 19th Amendment, guaranteeing women's right to vote, to the states for ratification.
Speaker of the House: Frederick H. Gillett (R–Massachusetts)
Majority Leader: Frank W. Mondell (R–Wyoming)
Minority Leader: James Beauchamp Clark (D–Missouri)
Democratic Caucus Chairman: Arthur G. DeWalt (D–Pennsylvania)
Republican Conference Chairman: Horace M. Towner (R–Iowa)
Clerk of the House: William Tyler Page

67TH CONGRESS (1921–1923)

435 Representatives
2 Delegates
131 Democrats
302 Republicans
Congressional Summary:

This Congress established the Veterans' Bureau.
Speaker of the House: Frederick H. Gillett (R–Massachusetts)
Majority Leader: Frank W. Mondell (R–Wyoming)
Minority Leader: Claude Kitchin (D–North Carolina)
Democratic Caucus Chairman: Sam Rayburn (D–Texas)
Republican Conference Chairman: Horace M. Towner (R–Iowa)
Clerk of the House: William Tyler Page

68TH CONGRESS (1923–1925)

435 Representatives
2 Delegates
207 Democrats
225 Republicans
Congressional Summary:

This Congress established the Foreign Service and also passed the Federal Corrupt Practices Act.
Speaker of the House: Frederick H. Gillett (R–Massachusetts)
Majority Leader: Nicholas Longworth (R–Ohio)
Minority Leader: Finis J. Garrett (D–Tennessee)

Democratic Caucus Chairman: Henry T. Rainey (D–Illinois)
Republican Conference Chairman: Sydney Anderson (R–Minnesota)
Clerk of the House: William Tyler Page

69TH CONGRESS (1925–1927)

435 Representatives
2 Delegates
183 Democrats
247 Republicans
Speaker of the House: Nicholas Longworth (R–Ohio)
Majority Leader: John Q. Tilson (R–Connecticut)
Minority Leader: Finis J. Garrett (D–Tennessee)
Democratic Caucus Chairman: Charles D. Carter (D–Oklahoma)
Republican Conference Chairman: Willis C. Hawley (R–Oregon)
Clerk of the House: William Tyler Page

70TH CONGRESS (1927–1929)

435 Representatives
2 Delegates
194 Democrats
238 Republicans
Congressional Summary:
    This Congress undertook natural resources initiatives including: flood control along the Mississippi River; a survey of national forest reserves; and a dam project along the Colorado River.
Speaker of the House: Nicholas Longworth (R–Ohio)
Majority Leader: John Q. Tilson (R–Connecticut)
Minority Leader: Finis J. Garrett (D–Tennessee)
Democratic Caucus Chairman: Arthur H. Greenwood (D–Indiana)
Republican Conference Chairman: Willis C. Hawley (R–Oregon)
Clerk of the House: William Tyler Page

71ST CONGRESS (1929–1931)

435 Representatives
2 Delegates
164 Democrats
270 Republicans
Congressional Summary:

This Congress enacted the Agricultural Marketing Act and the Smoot-Hawley Tariff after the October 1929 stock market crash. Congress established the Veterans' Administration as an independent agency and adopted the Star Spangled Banner as the national anthem.
Speaker of the House: Nicholas Longworth (R–Ohio)
Majority Leader: John Q. Tilson (R–Connecticut)
Minority Leader: John N. Garner (D–Texas)
Democratic Caucus Chairman: David H. Kincheloe (D–Kentucky)
Republican Conference Chairman: Willis C. Hawley (R–Oregon)
Clerk of the House: William Tyler Page

72ND CONGRESS (1931–1933)

435 Representatives
2 Delegates
216 Democrats
218 Republicans
Congressional Summary:
   This Congress established the Reconstruction Finance Corporation to provide loans to banks and industry. Congress refused the bonus payments World War I veterans had been promised.
Speaker of the House: John N. Garner (D–Texas)
Majority Leader: Henry T. Rainey (D–Illinois)
Minority Leader: Bertrand H. Snell (R–New York)
Democratic Caucus Chairman: William W. Arnold (D–Illinois)
Republican Conference Chairman: Willis C. Hawley (R–Oregon)
Clerk of the House: South Trimble

73RD CONGRESS (1933–1935)

435 Representatives
2 Delegates
313 Democrats
117 Republicans
Congressional Summary:
   This Congress controlled commercial banking, provided aid to farmers, and launched infrastructure projects. Other agencies created during this period: the Tennessee Valley Authority, the Securities and Exchange Commission, and the Federal Communications Commission.
Speaker of the House: Henry T. Rainey (D–Illinois)
Majority Leader: Joseph W. Byrns (D–Tennessee)
Minority Leader: Bertrand H. Snell (R–New York)

Democratic Caucus Chairman: Clarence F. Lea (D–California)
Republican Conference Chairman: Robert Luce (R–Massachusetts)
Clerk of the House: South Trimble

74TH CONGRESS (1935–1937)

435 Representatives
2 Delegates
322 Democrats
103 Republicans
Congressional Summary:
   This Congress encouraged collective bargaining, created Social Security, regulated public utilities, and passed the Neutrality Act.
Speaker of the House: Joseph W. Byrns (D–Tennessee); William B. Bankhead (D–Alabama)
Majority Leader: William B. Bankhead (D–Alabama)
Minority Leader: Bertrand H. Snell (R–New York)
Democratic Caucus Chairman: Edward T. Taylor (D–Colorado)
Republican Conference Chairman: Frederick R. Lehlbach (R–New Jersey)
Clerk of the House: South Trimble

75TH CONGRESS (1937–1939)

435 Representatives
2 Delegates
334 Democrats
88 Republicans
Congressional Summary:
   This Congress passed New Deal legislation, including farm and housing loan programs and new minimum wage standards. Congress also regulated crop and natural gas production, civilian aviation, and food and drug ads.
Speaker of the House: William B. Bankhead (D–Alabama)
Majority Leader: Sam Rayburn (D–Texas)
Minority Leader: Bertrand H. Snell (R–New York)
Democratic Caucus Chairman: Robert L. Doughton (D–North Carolina)
Republican Conference Chairman: Roy O. Woodruff (R–Michigan)
Clerk of the House: South Trimble

76TH CONGRESS (1939–1941)

435 Representatives
2 Delegates

262 Democrats
169 Republicans
Congressional Summary:

This Congress also passed internal security measures that required foreign nationals to register with federal authorities and established the first peacetime draft.

Speaker of the House: Sam Rayburn (D–Texas); William B. Bankhead (D–Alabama)
Majority Leader: John W. McCormack (D–Massachusetts); Sam Rayburn (D–Texas)
Minority Leader: Joseph W. Martin, Jr. (R–Massachusetts)
Democratic Caucus Chairman: John W. McCormack (D–Massachusetts)
Republican Conference Chairman: Roy O. Woodruff (R–Michigan)
Clerk of the House: South Trimble

77TH CONGRESS (1941–1943)

435 Representatives
2 Delegates
267 Democrats
162 Republicans
Congressional Summary:

After the Japanese bombed Pearl Harbor, this Congress declared war on the Axis Powers.

Speaker of the House: Sam Rayburn (D–Texas)
Majority Leader: John W. McCormack (D–Massachusetts)
Minority Leader: Joseph W. Martin, Jr. (R–Massachusetts)
Democratic Caucus Chairman: Richard M. Duncan (D–Missouri)
Republican Conference Chairman: Roy O. Woodruff (R–Michigan)
Clerk of the House: South Trimble

78TH CONGRESS (1943–1945)

435 Representatives
2 Delegates
222 Democrats
209 Republicans
Congressional Summary:

This Congress repealed the Chinese Exclusion Acts and authorized absentee voting. Congress also established the system of veterans' preference for government jobs and the G.I. Bill of Rights.

Speaker of the House: Sam Rayburn (D–Texas)

Majority Leader: John W. McCormack (D–Massachusetts)
Minority Leader: Joseph W. Martin, Jr. (R–Massachusetts); Leslie C. Arends (R–Illinois)
Democratic Caucus Chairman: Harry R. Sheppard (D–California)
Republican Conference Chairman: Roy O. Woodruff (R–Michigan)
Clerk of the House: South Trimble

79TH CONGRESS (1945–1947)

435 Representatives
2 Delegates
242 Democrats
191 Republicans
Congressional Summary:
   Congress instituted the Fulbright scholars program. Congress also enacted full employment legislation, new airports and hospitals.
Speaker of the House: Sam Rayburn (D–Texas)
Majority Leader: John W. McCormack (D–Massachusetts)
Minority Leader: Joseph W. Martin, Jr. (R–Massachusetts)
Democratic Caucus Chairman: Jere Cooper (D–Tennessee)
Republican Conference Chairman: Roy O. Woodruff (R–Michigan)
Clerk of the House: South Trimble

80TH CONGRESS (1947–1949)

435 Representatives
2 Delegates
188 Democrats
246 Republicans
Congressional Summary:
   This Congress sent to the states for ratification a constitutional amendment limiting Presidents to two terms. Congress also authorized economic and military aid to countries, it passed the Marshall Plan, created the National Security Council and the Central Intelligence Agency.
Speaker of the House: Joseph W. Martin, Jr. (R–Massachusetts)
Majority Leader: Charles A. Halleck (R–Indiana)
Minority Leader: Sam Rayburn (D–Texas)
Democratic Caucus Chairman: Aime J. Forand (D–Rhode Island)
Republican Conference Chairman: Roy O. Woodruff (R–Michigan)
Clerk of the House: John Andrews

81ST CONGRESS (1949–1951)

435 Representatives
2 Delegates
263 Democrats
171 Republicans
Congressional Summary:
This Congress enacted internal security legislation; it also approved U.S. entry in the North Atlantic Treaty Organization.
Speaker of the House: Sam Rayburn (D–Texas)
Majority Leader: John W. McCormack (D–Massachusetts)
Minority Leader: Joseph W. Martin, Jr. (R–Massachusetts)
Democratic Caucus Chairman: Francis E. Walter (D–Pennsylvania)
Republican Conference Chairman: Roy O. Woodruff (R–Michigan)
Clerk of the House: Ralph R. Roberts

82ND CONGRESS (1951–1953)

435 Representatives
2 Delegates
235 Democrats
199 Republicans
Congressional Summary:
This Congress passed a GI Bill for Korean veterans and the restrictive McCarran–Walter immigration act.
Speaker of the House: Sam Rayburn (D–Texas)
Majority Leader: John W. McCormack (D–Massachusetts)
Minority Leader: Joseph W. Martin, Jr. (R–Massachusetts)
Democratic Caucus Chairman: Jere Cooper (D–Tennessee)
Republican Conference Chairman: Clifford R. Hope (R–Kansas)
Clerk of the House: Ralph R. Roberts

NOTE

1. Source: *History, Art & Archives, U.S. House of Representatives*, "51st-82nd Congress," http://history.house.gov/Congressional-Overview/Profiles/51st/ (May 11, 2014).

Appendix B

Southern Democratic Senators, 51st–82nd Congress[1]

51ST CONGRESS (1889–1891)

Barbour, John Strode, Jr. VA
Bate, William Brimage TN
Beck, James Burnie KY
Berry, James AR
Blackburn, Joseph KY
Brown, Joseph GA
Butler, Matthew SC
Call, Wilkinson FL
Carlisle, John KY
Coke, Richard TX
Colquitt, Alfred GA
Daniel, John VA
Eustis, James LA
George, James MS
Gibson, Randall LA
Hampton, Wade SC
Harris, Isham TN
Jones, James AR
Morgan, John AL
Pasco, Samuel FL
Pugh, James AL
Ransom, Matt NC
Reagan, John TX

Vance, Zebulon NC
Walthall, Edward MS

52ND CONGRESS (1891–1893)

Barbour, John VA
Bate, William TN
Berry, James AR
Blackburn, Joseph KY
Buttler, Matthew SC
Caffery, Donelson LA
Call, Wilkinson FL
Carlisle, John KY
Chilton, Horace TX
Coke, Richard TX
Colquitt, Alfred GA
Daniel, John VA
George, James MS
Gibson, Randall LA
Gordon, John GA
Gray, George DE
Harris, Isham TN
Hunton, Eppa VA
Irby, John SC
Jones, James AR
Lindsay, William KY
Mills, Roger TX
Morgan, John AL
Pasco, Samuel FL
Pugh, James AL
Ransom, Matt NC
Reagan, John TX
Vance, Zebulon NC
Walthall, Edward MS
White, Edward LA

53RD CONGRESS (1893–1895)

Bate, William TN
Berry, James AR
Blackburn, Joseph KY
Blanchard, Newton LA

Butler, Matthew SC
Caffery, Donelson LA
Call, Wilkinson FL
Coke, Richard TX
Colquitt, Alfred GA
Daniel, John VA
George, James MS
Gordon, John GA
Harris, Isham TN
Hunton, Eppa VA
Irby, John SC
Jarvis, Thomas NC
Jones, James AR
Lindsay, William KY
Martin, John KS
McLaurin, Anselm MS
Mills, Roger TX
Morgan, John AL
Pasco, Samuel FL
Pugh, James AL
Ransom, Matt NC
Vance, Zebulon NC
Walsh, Patrick GA
Walthall, Edward MS
White, Edward LA

54TH CONGRESS (1895–1897)

Bacon, Augustus GA
Bate, William TN
Berry, James AR
Blackburn, Joseph KY
Blanchard, Newton LA
Caffery, Donelson LA
Call, Wilkinson FL
Chilton, Horace TX
Daniel, John VA
George, James MS
Gordon, John GA
Harris, Isham TN
Irby, John SC
Jones, James AR

Lindsay, William KY
Martin, Thomas VA
Mills, Roger TX
Morgan, John AL
Pasco, Samuel FL
Pugh, James AL
Tillman, Benjamin SC
Walthall, Edward MS

55TH CONGRESS (1897–1899)

Bacon, Augustus GA
Bate, William TN
Berry, James AR
Carrery, Donelson LA
Chilton, Horace TX
Clay, Alexander GA
Daniel, John VA
Earle, Joseph SC
George, James MS
Harris, Isham TN
Jones, James AR
Lindsay, William KY
Mallory, Stephen FL
Martin, Thomas VA
McEnery, Samuel LA
McLaurin, John SC
Mills, Roger TX
Money, Hernando MS
Morgan, John AL
Pasco, Samuel FL
Pettus, Edmund AL
Sullivan, William MS
Tillman, Benjamin SC
Turley, Thomas TN
Walthall, Edward MS

56TH CONGRESS (1899–1901)

Bacon, Augustus GA
Bate, William TN
Berry, James AR

Caffery, Donelson LA
Chilton, Horace TX
Clay, Alexander GA
Culberson, Charles TX
Daniel, John VA
Jones, James AR
Lindsay, William KY
Mallory, Stephen FL
Martin, Thomas VA
McEnery, Samuel LA
McLaurin, John SC
Money, Hernando MS
Morgan, John AL
Pasco, Samuel FL
Pettus, Edmund AL
Sullivan, William MS
Taliaferro, James FL
Tillman, Benjamin SC
Turley, Thomas TN

57TH CONGRESS (1901–1903)

Bacon, Augustus GA
Bailey, Joseph TX
Bate, William TN
Berry, James AR
Blackburn, Joseph KY
Carmack, Edward TN
Clay, Alexander GA
Culberson, Charles TX
Daniel, John VA
Foster, Murphy LA
Jones, James AR
Mallory, Stephen FL
Martin, Thomas VA
McEnery, Samuel LA
McLaurin, Anselm MS
McLaurin, John SC
Money, Hernando MS
Morgan, John AL
Pettus, Edmund AL
Simmons, Furnifold NC

Taliaferro, James FL
Tillman, Benjamin SC

58TH CONGRESS (1903–1905)

Bacon, Augustus GA
Bailey, Joseph TX
Bate, William TN
Berry, James AR
Blackburn, Joseph KY
Carmack, Edward TN
Clarke, James AR
Clay, Alexander GA
Culberson, Charles TX
Daniel, John VA
Foster, Murphy LA
Latimer, Asbury SC
Mallory, Stephen FL
Martin, Thomas VA
McCreary, James KY
McEnery, Samuel LA
McLaurin, Anselm MS
Money, Hernando MS
Morgan, John AL
Overman, Lee NC
Pettus, Edmund AL
Simmons, Furnifold NC
Taliaferro, James FL
Tillman, Benjamin SC

59TH CONGRESS (1905–1907)

Bacon, Augustus GA
Bailey, Joseph TX
Bate, William TN
Berry, James AR
Blackburn, Joseph KY
Carmack, Edward TN
Clarke, James AR
Clay, Alexander GA
Culberson, Charles TX
Daniel, John VA

Foster, Murphy LA
Frazier, James TN
Latimer, Asbury SC
Mallory, Stephen FL
Martin, Thomas VA
McCreary, James KY
McEnery, Samuel LA
McLaurin, Anselm MS
Money, Hernando MS
Morgan, John AL
Overman, Lee NC
Pettus, Edmund AL
Simmons, Furnifold NC
Taliaferro, James FL
Tillman, Benjamin SC

60TH CONGRESS (1907–1909)

Bacon, Augustus GA
Bailey, Joseph TX
Bankhead, John AL
Bryan, William FL
Clarke, James AR
Clay, Alexander GA
Culberson, Charles TX
Daniel, John VA
Davis, Jess AR
Foster, Murphy LA
Frazier, James TN
Gary, Frank SC
Johnston, Joseph AL
Latimer, Asbury SC
Martin, Thomas VA
McCreary, James KY
McEnery, Samuel LA
McLaurin, Anselm MS
Milton, William FL
Money, Hernando MS
Morgan, John AL
Overman, Lee NC
Owen, Robert OK
Paynter, Thomas KY

Pettus, Edmund AL
Simmons, Furnifold NC
Taliaferro, James FL
Taylor, Robert TN
Tillman, Benjamin SC

61st CONGRESS (1909–1911)

Bacon, Augustus GA
Bailey, Joseph TX
Bankhead, John AL
Clarke, James AR
Clay, Alexander GA
Culberson, Charles TX
Daniel, John VA
Davis, Jeff AR
Fletcher, Duncan FL
Foster, Murphy LA
Frazier, James TN
Gordon, James MS
Gore, Thomas OK
Johnston, Joseph AL
Martin, Thomas VA
McEnery, Samuel LA
McLaurin, Anselm MS
Money, Henrando MS
Overman, Lee NC
Owen, Robert OK
Paynter, Thomas KY
Percy, Le Roy MS
Simmons, Furnifold NC
Smith, Ellison SC
Swanson, Claude VA
Taliaferro, James FL
Taylor, Robert TN
Terrell, Joseph GA
Thornton, John LA
Tillman, Benjamin SC

62nd CONGRESS (1911–1913)

Bacon, Augustus GA

Bailey, Joseph TX
Bankhead, John AL
Bryan, Nathan FL
Clarke, James AR
Culberson, Charles TX
Davis, Jeff AR
Fletcher, Duncan FL
Foster, Murphy LA
Frazier, James TN
Gore, Thomas OK
Heiskell, John AR
Johnston, Joseph AL
Johnston, Rienzi TX
Kavanaugh, William AR
Lea, Luke TN
Martin, Thomas VA
Overman, Lee NC
Owen, Robert OK
Paynter, Thomas KY
Percy, Le Roy MS
Sherppard, Morris TX
Simmons, Furnifold NC
Smith, Ellison SC
Smith, Hoke GA
Swanson, Claude VA
Taylor, Robert TN
Terrell, Joseph GA
Thornton, John LA
Tillman, Benjamin SC

63RD CONGRESS (1913–1915)

Bacon, Augustus GA
Bankhead, John AL
Bryan, Nathan FL
Camden, Johnson KY
Clarke, James AR
Culberson, Charles TX
Fletcher, Duncan FL
Gore, Thomas OK
Hardwick, Thomas GA
James, Ollie KY

Johnston, Joseph AL
Lea, Luke TN
Martin, Thomas VA
Overman, Lee NC
Owen, Robert OK
Ransdell, Joseph LA
Robinson, Joseph AR
Sheppard, Morris TX
Shields, John TN
Simmons, Furnifold NC
Smith, Ellison SC
Smith, Hoke GA
Swanson, Claude VA
Thompson, William KS
Thornton, John LA
Tillman, Benjamin SC
Vardaman, James MS
West, William GA
White, Francis AL
Williams, John MS

64TH CONGRESS (1915–1917)

Bankhead, John AL
Beckham, John KY
Broussard, Robert LA
Bryan, Nathan FL
Clarke, James AR
Culberson, Charles TX
Fletcher, Duncan FL
Gore, Thomas OK
Hardwick, Thomas GA
James, Ollie KY
Kirby, William AR
Lea, Luke TN
Martin, Thomas VA
Overman, Lee NC
Owen, Robert OK
Ransdell, Joseph LA
Robinson, Joseph AR
Sheppard, Morris TX
Shields, John TN

Simmons, Furnifold NC
Smith, Ellison SC
Smith, Hoke GA
Swanson, Claude VA
Thompson, William KS
Tillman, Benjamin SC
Underwood, Oscar AL
Vardaman, James MS
Williams, John MS

65TH CONGRESS (1917–1919)

Bankhead, John AL
Beckham, John KY
Benet, Christie SC
Broussard, Robert LA
Culberson, Charles TX
Fletcher, Duncan FL
Gay, Edward LA
Gore, Thomas OK
Guion, Walter LA
Hardwick, Thomas GA
James, Ollie KY
Kirby, William AR
Martin, George KY
Martin, Thomas VA
McKellar, Kenneth TN
Overman, Lee NC
Owen, Robert OK
Pollock, William SC
Ransdell, Joseph LA
Robinson, Joseph AR
Sheppard, Morris TX
Shields, John TN
Simmons, Furnifold NC
Smith, Ellison SC
Smith, Hoke GA
Swanson, Claude VA
Tillman, Benjamin SC
Trammell, Park FL
Underwood, Oscar AL
Vardaman, James MS

Williams, John MS

66TH CONGRESS (1919–1921)

Bankhead, John AL
Beckham, John KY
Comer, Braxton AL
Culberson, Charles TX
Dial, Nathaniel SC
Fletcher, Duncan FL
Gay, Edward LA
Glass, Carter VA
Harris, William GA
Harrison, Byron MS
Heflin, James AL
Kirby, William AR
Martin, Thomas VA
McKellar, Kenneth TN
Overman, Lee NC
Owen, Robert OK
Ransdell, Joseph LA
Robinson, Joseph AR
Sheppard, Morris TX
Shields, John TN
Simmons, Furnifold NC
Smith, Ellison SC
Smith, Hoke GA
Stanley, Augustus KY
Swanson, Claude VA
Trammell, Park FL
Underwood, Oscar AL
Williams, John MS

67TH CONGRESS (1921–1923)

Broussard, Edwin LA
Caraway, Thaddeus AR
Culberson, Charles TX
Dial, Nathaniel SC
Felton, Rebecca GA
Fletcher, Duncan FL
George, Walter, GA

Glass, Carter VA
Harris, William GA
Harrison, Byron MS
Heflin, James AL
McKellar, Kenneth TN
Overman, Lee NC
Owen, Robert OK
Ransdell, Joseph LA
Robinson, Joseph AR
Sheppard, Morris TX
Shields, John TN
Simmons, Furnifold NC
Smith, Ellison SC
Stanley, Augustus KY
Swanson, Claude VA
Trammell, Park FL
Underwood, Oscar AL
Watson, Thomas GA

68TH CONGRESS (1923–1925)

Broussard, Edwin LA
Caraway, Thaddeus AR
Dial, Nathanial SC
Fletcher, Duncan FL
George, Walter GA
Glass, Carter VA
Harris, William GA
Harrison, Byron MS
Heflin, James AL
Mayfield, Earle TX
McKellar, Kenneth TN
Overman, Lee NC
Owen, Robert OK
Ransdell, Joseph LA
Robinson, Joseph AR
Sheppard, Morris TX
Shields, John TN
Simmons, Furnifold NC
Smith, Ellison SC
Stanley, Augustus KY
Stephens, Hubert MS

Swanson, Claude VA
Trammell, Park FL
Underwood, Oscar AL

69TH CONGRESS (1925–1927)

Blease, Coleman SC
Broussard, Edwin LA
Caraway, Thaddeus AR
Fletcher, Duncan FL
George, Walter
Glass, Carter VA
Harris, William GA
Harrison, Byron MS
Heflin, James AL
Mayfield, Earle TX
McKellar, Kenneth TN
Overman, Lee NC
Ransdell, Joseph LA
Robinson, Joseph AR
Sheppard, Morris TX
Simmons, Furnifold NC
Smith, Ellison SC
Stephens, Hubert MS
Swanson, Claude VA
Trammell, Park FL
Tyson, Lawrence TN
Underwood, Oscar Al

70TH CONGRESS (1927–1929)

Barkely, Alben KY
Black, Hugo AL
Blease, Coleman SC
Broussard LA
Caraway, Thaddeus AR
Fletcher, Duncan FL
George, Walter GA
Glass, Carter VA
Harris, William GA
Harrison, Byron MS
Heflin, James AL

Mayfield, Earle TX
McKellar, Kenneth TN
Overman, Lee NC
Ransdell, Joseph LA
Robinson, Joseph AR
Sheppard, Morris TX
Simmons, Furnifold NC
Smith, Ellison SC
Stephens, Hubert MS
Swanson, Claude VA
Thomas, Elmer OK
Thomas, John OK
Trammell, Park FL
Tyson, Lawrence TN

71st CONGRESS (1929–1931)

Barkley, Alben KY
Black, Hugo AL
Blease, Coleman SC
Brock, William TN
Broussard, Edwin LA
Caraway, Thaddeus AR
Connally, Thomas TX
Fletcher, Duncan FL
George, Walter GA
Glass, Carter VA
Harris, William GA
Harrison, Byron MS
Heflin, James AL
McKellar, Kenneth TN
Morrison, Cameron NC
Overman, Lee NC
Ransdell, Joseph LA
Robinson, Joseph AR
Sheppard, Morris TX
Simmons, Furnifold NC
Smith, Ellison SC
Stephens, Hubert MS
Swanson, Claude VA
Thomas, Elmer OK
Thomas, John OK

Trammell, Park FL
Tyson, Lawrence TN

72ND CONGRESS (1931–1933)

Bachman, Nathan TN
Bailey, Josiah NC
Bankhead, John AL
Barkley, Alben KY
Black, Hugo AL
Broussard, Edwin LA
Byrnes, James SC
Caraway, Hattie AR
Caraway, Thaddeus AR
Cohen, John GA
Connally, Thomas TX
Fletcher, Duncan FL
George, Walter GA
Glass, Carter VA
Gore, Thomas OK
Harris, William GA
Harrison, Byron MS
Hull, Cordell TN
Logan, Marvel KY
Long, Huey LA
McKellar, Kenneth TN
Morrison, Cameron NC
Reynolds, Robert NC
Robinson, Joseph AR
Russell, Richard GA
Sheppard, Morris TX
Smith, Ellison SC
Stephens, Hubert MS
Swanson, Claude VA
Thomas, Elmer OK
Thomas, John OK
Trammell, Park FL

73RD CONGRESS (1933–1935)

Bachman, Nathan TN
Bailey, Josiah NC

Bankhead, John AL
Barkley, Alben KY
Black, Hugo AL
Byrd, Harry VA
Byrnes, James SC
Caraway, Hattie AR
Connally, Thomas TX
Fletcher, Duncan FL
George, Walter GA
Glass, Carter VA
Gore, Thomas OK
Harrison, Byron MS
Logan, Marvel KY
Long, Huey LA
McGill, George KS
McKellar, Kenneth TN
Overton, John LA
Reynolds, Robert NC
Robinson, Joseph AR
Russell, Richard GA
Sheppard, Morris TX
Smith, Ellison SC
Stephens, Hubert MS
Thomas, Elmer OK
Thomas, John OK
Trammell, Park FL

74TH CONGRESS (1935–1937)

Andrews, Charles FL
Bachman, Nathan TN
Bailey, Josiah NC
Bankhead, John AL
Barkley, Alben KY
Bilbo, Theodore MS
Black, Hugo AL
Byrd, Harry VA
Byrnes, James SC
Caraway, Hattie AR
Connally, Thomas TX
Fletcher, Duncan FL
George, Walter GA

Appendix B

Glass, Carter VA
Gore, Thomas OK
Harrison, Byron MS
Hill, William FL
Loftin, Scott FL
Logan, Marvel KY
Long, Huey LA
Long, Rose LA
McKellar, Kenneth TN
Overton, John LA
Pepper, Claude FL
Reynolds, Robert NC
Robinson, Joseph AR
Russell, Richard GA
Sheppard, Morris TX
Smith, Ellison SC
Thomas, Elmer OK
Thomas, John OK
Trammell, Park FL

75TH CONGRESS (1937–1939)

Andrews, Charles FL
Bachman, Nathan TN
Bailey, Josiah NC
Bankhead, John AL
Barkley, Alben KY
Berry,George TN
Bilbo, Theodore MS
Black, Hugo AL
Byrd, Harry VA
Byrnes, James SC
Caraway, Hattie AR
Connally, Thomas TX
Ellender, Allen LA
George, Walter GA
Glass, Carter VA
Graves, Dixie AL
Harrison, Byron MS
Hill, Joseph AL
Lee, Joshua OK
Logan, Marvel KY

McKellar, Kenneth TN
Miller, John AR
Overton, John LA
Pepper, Claude FL
Reynolds, Robert NC
Robinson, Joseph AR
Russell, Richard GA
Sheppard, Morris TX
Smith, Ellison SC
Thomas, Elmer OK
Thomas, John OK

76TH CONGRESS (1939–1941)

Andrews, Charles FL
Bailey, Josiah NC
Bankhead, John AL
Barkley, Alben KY
Bilbo, Theodore MS
Byrd, Harry VA
Byrnes, James SC
Caraway, Hattie AR
Chandler, Albert KY
Connally, Thomas TX
Ellender, Allen LA
George, Walter GA
Glass, Carter VA
Harrison, Byron MS
Hill, Joseph AL
Lee, Joshua OK
Logan, Marvel KY
McKellar, Kenneth TN
Miller, John AR
Overton, John LA
Pepper, Claude FL
Reynolds, Robert NC
Russell, Richard GA
Sheppard, Morris
Smith, Ellison SC
Stewart, Arthur TN
Thomas, Elmer OK
Thomas, John OK

77TH CONGRESS (1941–1943)

Andrews, Charles FL
Bailey, Josiah NC
Bankhead, John AL
Barkley, Alben KY
Bilbo, Theodore MS
Byrd, Harry VA
Byrnes, James SC
Caraway, Hattie AR
Chandler, Albert KY
Connally, Thomas TX
Doxey, Wall MS
Eastland, James MS
Ellender, Allen LA
George, Walter GA
Glass, Carter VA
Harrison, Byron MS
Hill, Joseph AL
Houston, Andrew TX
Lee, Joshua OK
Lumpkin, Alva SC
Maybank, Burnet SC
McKellar, Kenneth TN
Miller, John AR
O'Daniel, Wilbert TX
Overton, John LA
Peace, Roger SC
Pepper, Claude FL
Reynolds, Robert NC
Russell, Richard GA
Sheppard, Morris TX
Smith, Ellison SC
Spencer, George AR
Stewart, Arthur TN
Thomas, Elmer, OK
Thomas, John OK

78TH CONGRESS (1943–1945)

Andrews, Charles FL
Bailey, Josiah NC

Bankhead, John AL
Barkley, Alben KY
Bilbo, Theodore MS
Byrd, Harry VA
Caraway, Hattie AR
Chandler, Albert KY
Connally, Thomas TX
Eastland, James MS
Ellender, Allen LA
George, Walter GA
Glass, Carter VA
Hall, Wilton SC
Hill, Joseph AL
Maybank, Burnet SC
McClellan, John AR
McKellar, Kenneth TN
O'Daniel, Wilbert TX
Overton, John LA
Pepper, Claude FL
Reynolds, Robert NC
Russell, Richard GA
Smith, Ellison SC
Stewart, Arthur TN
Thomas, Elmer OK
Thomas, John OK

79TH CONGRESS (1945–1947)

Andrews, Charles FL
Bailey, Josiah NC
Bankhead, John AL
Barkley, Alben KY
Bilbo, Theodore MS
Burch, Thomas VA
Byrd, Harry VA
Chandler, Albert KY
Connally, Thomas TX
Eastland, James MS
Ellender, Allen LA
Fulbright, James AR
George, Walter GA
Glass, Carter VA

Hill, Joseph AL
Hoey, Clyde NC
Holland, Spessard FL
Johnston, Olin SC
Maybank, Burnet SC
McClellan, John AR
McKellar, Kenneth TN
O'Daniel, Wilbert TX
Overton, John LA
Pepper, Claude FL
Robertson, Absalom VA
Russell, Richard GA
Sparkman, John AL
Stewart, Arthur TN
Swift, George AL
Thomas, Elmer OK
Thomas, John OK
Umstead, William NC

80TH CONGRESS (1947–1949)

Barkley, Alben KY
Bilbo, Theodore MS
Broughton, Joseph NC
Byrd, Harry VA
Connally, Thomas TX
Eastland, James MS
Ellender, Allen LA
Feazel, William LA
Fulbright, James AR
George, Walter GA
Hoey, Clyde NC
Holland, Spessard FL
Johnston, Olin SC
Long, Russell
Maybank, Burnet SC
McClellan, John AR
McKellar, Kenneth TN
O'Daniel, Wilbert TX
Overton, John LA
Pepper, Claude FL
Robertson, Absalom VA

Russell, Richard GA
Sparkman, John AL
Stennis, John MS
Stewart, Arthur TN
Thomas, Elmer OK
Thomas, John OK
Umstead, William NC

81ST CONGRESS (1949–1951)

Barkley, Alben KY
Broughton, Joseph NC
Byrd, Harry VA
Chapman, Virgil KY
Clements, Earle KY
Connally, Thomas TX
Eastland, James MS
Ellender, Allen LA
Fulbright, James AR
George, Walter GA
Graham, Frank NC
Hill, Joseph AL
Hoey, Clyde NC
Holland, Spessard FL
Johnson, Lyndon TX
Johnston, Olin SC
Kefauver, Carey TN
Kerr, Robert OK
Long, Russell LA
Maybank, Burnet SC
McClellan, John AR
McKellar, Kenneth TN
Pepper, Claude FL
Robertson, Absalom VA
Russell, Richard GA
Smith, Willis NC
Sparkman, John AL
Stennis, John MS
Thomas, Elmer OK
Thomas, John OK
Withers, Garrett KY

82ND CONGRESS (1951–1953)

Byrd, Harry VA
Chapman, Virgil KY
Clements, Earle KY
Connally, Thomas TX
Eastland, James MS
Ellender, Allen LA
Fulbright, James AR
George, Walter GA
Hill, Joseph AL
Hoey, Clyde NC
Holland, Spessard FL
Johnson, Lyndon TX
Johnston, Olin SC
Kefauver, Carey TN
Kerr, Robert OK
Long, Russell LA
Maybank, Burnet SC
McClellan, John AR
McKellar, Kenneth TN
Monroney, Almer OK
Robertson, Absalom VA
Russell, Richard GA
Smathers, George
Smith, Willis NC
Sparkman, John AL
Stennis, John MS
Underwood, Thomas KY

NOTE

1. Biographical Directory of the United States Congress, 1774-present, http://www.senate.gov/pagelayout/history/h_multi_sections_and_teasers/Biographical_Directory.htm

Selected Bibliography

"Activists in Congress." *The Reflector*, June 30, 1934.

Adrian, Charles R. *State and Local Governments*. 2nd ed. New York: McGraw-Hill, 1967.

"A Look at Federal Role in Civil Rights Cases." *Daily Herald (Arlington Heights, IL)*, August 19, 2013.

Allen, Howard W. and Jerome M. Clubb. *Race, Class, and the Death Penalty: Capital Punishment in American History*. Albany, NY: SUNY Press, 2009.

Allen, James and Others, *Without Sanctuary: Lynching Photography in America*. Santa Fe, NM: Twin Palms Publishers: 2000.

Apel, Dora. *Imagery of Lynching: Black Men, White Women, and the Mob*. New Brunswick, NJ: Rutgers University Press, 2004.

Anreus, Alejandro, Diana L. Linden, and Jonathan Weinberg, eds. *The Social and the Real: Political Art of the 1930s in the Western Hemisphere*. University Park, PA: Penn State Press, 2006.

Arenberg, Richard A. and Robert B. Dove. *Defending the Filibuster: The Soul of the Senate*. Bloomington, IN: Indiana University Press, 2012.

Armstrong, Julie Buckner. *Mary Turner and the Memory of Lynching*. Athens, GA: University of Georgia Press, 2011.

Babbitt, Susan E., and Sue Campbell, eds. *Racism and Philosophy*. Ithaca, NY: Cornell University Press, 1999.

Barber, Sotirios A. *The Fallacies of States' Rights*. Cambridge, MA: Harvard University Press, 2013.

Barrows, Samuel J. "Legislative Tendencies as to Capital Punishment." *Annals of the American Academy of Political and Social Science* 29 (1907): 178-181.

Bartley, Numan V., ed. *The Evolution of Southern Culture*. Athens: University of Georgia Press, 1988.

Beale, Joseph H, Jr. "Retreat from a Murderous Assault." *Harvard Law Review* 16 (1903): 567-582.

Belleslies, Michael A. ed. *Lethal Imagination: Violence and Brutality in American History*. New York: NYU Press, 1999.

Berg, Manfred. *Popular Justice: A History of Lynching in America*. Lanham, MD: Ivan R. Dee, 2011.

Benson, Godfrey and Baron Charnwood. *Theodore Roosevelt*. University of Michigan: Atlantic Monthly Press, 1913).

Bernstein, Patricia. *The First Waco Horror: The Lynching of Jesse Washington and the Rise of the NAACP*. College Station, TX: Texas A&M University Press, 2006.

Bessler, John D. *Legacy of Violence: Lynch Mobs and Executions in Minnesota*. Minneapolis, MN: University of Minnesota Press, 2003.

Beth, Richard S. *Filibusters and Cloture in the Senate*. Darby, PA: DIANE Publishing, 2010.

Binder, Sarah A. *Politics or Principle? Filibustering in the United States Senate*. Washington, DC: Brookings Institution Press, 1997.

Black, Earl, and Merle Black. *The Rise of Southern Republicans*. Cambridge, MA: Belknap Press, 2003.

Black, Henry C. *Handbook of American Constitutional Law*, 3d ed. St. Paul, MN: West Publishing Company, 1910.

Blassingame, John W. and John R. McKivigan. *The Frederick Douglass Papers: Series One; Speeches, Debates, and Interviews; Vol.5, 1881-1895*. New Haven: Yale University Press, 1992.

Blee, Kathleen M. *Women of the Klan: Racism and Gender in the 1920s*. Berkeley, CA: University of California Press, 1991.

Brennan Jr., William. "State Constitutions and the Protection of Individual Rights." *Harvard Law Review* 90 (1977): 489.

Brown, Nikki L M., and Barry M. Stentiford, eds. *The Jim Crow Encyclopedia*. The American Mosaic. Westport, Conn.: Greenwood Press, 2008.

Brown, Richard Maxwell. *Strain of Violence: Historical Studies of American Violence and Vigilantism*. New York: Oxford University Press, 1975.

Brown Wyatt, Bertram. *Southern Honor: Ethics and Behavior in the Old South*. New York: Oxford University Press, 1982.

Brundage, William F. *Lynching in the New South: Georgia and Virginia, 1880-1930*. Champaign, IL: University of Illinois Press, 1993.

Budiansky, Steven. *The Bloody Shirt: Terror after the Civil War*. New York: Plume. 2008.

Burton, Theodore E. "Development of the Federal Government." *Annals of the American Academy of Political and Social Science* 32 (1908): 212-217.

Camfield, David. "Racism Yardstick: It's All about Oppression." Winnipeg Free Press. September 3, 2013.

Capeci, Dominic J. *The Lynching of Cleo Wright*. Lexington, KY: University of Kentucky Press, 1998.

Carrigan, William D. *The Making of a Lynching Culture: Violence and Vigilantism in Central Texas, 1836-1916*. Champaign, IL: University of Illinois Press, 2006.

Chadbourn, James. *Lynching and the Law*. Clark, NJ: The Lawbook Exchange, Ltd., 2008.

Charland, Maurice. "Constitutive Rhetoric: The Case of the Peuple Quebecois." *Quarterly Journal of Speech* 73 (1987): 133-150.

Ciuba, Gary M. *Desire, Violence, and Divinity in Modern Southern Fiction: Katherine Anne Porter, Flannery O ' connor, Cormac Mccarthy, Walker Percy (Southern Literary Studies)*. Reprint ed. Baton Rouge, LA: Louisiana State University Press, 2011.

Clark, Champ. "Cloture." *The North American Review* 201 (1915): 516-520.

Collins, Charles W. *The 14th Amendment and the States: A Study of the Operation of the Restraint Clause of Section One of the 14th Amendment to the Constitution of the U.S.* Boston, MA: Little, Brown, 1912.

Committee, Democratic National. *The Campaign Text Book of the Democratic Party for the Presidential Election of 1892 (Classic Reprint)*. London: Forgotten Books, 2012.

Cooper, Jr., John Milton. *Woodrow Wilson: a Biography*. New York: Vintage, 2011.

Cooper, Joseph. "The Puzzle of Distrust." In *Congress and the Decline of Public Trust*, edited by Joseph Cooper. Boulder, CO: Westview Press, 1999.

Corwin, Edward. "The Supreme Court and the Fourteenth Amendment," in *American Constitutional History: Essays by Edward S. Corwin*, edited by Alpheus T. Mason and Gerald Garvey. New York, Evanston, and London: Harper and Row, 1964.

Curriden, Mark and Leroy Phillips. *Contempt of Court: The Turn of the Century Lynching that Launched a Hundred Years of Federalism*. New York: Anchor, 2001.

Curry, Tommy J. "The Fortune of Wells: Ida B. Wells-Barnett's Use of T. Thomas Fortune's Philosophy of Social Agitation as a Prolegomenon to Militant Civil Rights Activism," *Transactions of the Charles S. Peirce Society* 48 (2012): 456-482.

Cutler, James. *Lynch Law: An Investigation into the History of Lynching in the United States.* New York: Longmans, Green and Co., 1905.

Cutter, George W. "Race Prejudice." *The Advocate of Peace (1894-1920)* 73 (1911): 233-235.

Day, Ken Gonzales. *Lynching in the West, 1850-1935.* Durham, NC: Duke University Press, 2006.

Daugherty, H.M. "Respect for Law," *American Bar Association Journal* 7 (1921), 505-511.

DeSantis, Alan D. "Selling the American Dream to Black Southerners: The Chicago Defender and the Great Migration of 1915–1919." *Western Journal of Communications* 62 (1998): 477-79.

Dodd, Lawrence C. "A Theory of Congressional Cycles- Solving the Puzzle of Change." In *Congress and Policy Change*, edited by Gerald C. Wright, Jr., Leroy N. Rieselbach, and Lawrence C. Dodd. New York: Agathon, 1986.

Drachman, Edward R. and Robert Langran. *You Decide: Controversial Cases in American Politics.* Lanham, MD: Rowman & Littlefield, 2008.

Dray, Philip. *At the Hands of Persons Unknown: The Lynching of Black America.* New York: Random House, 2002.

"Drive on Filibuster Opened in Senate on Truman Order." *The New York Times*, March 1, 1949.

DuBois, W. E. Burghardt. "The Relation of the Negroes to the Whites in the South." *Annals of the American Academy of Political and Social Science* 18 (1901): 121-140.

DuRocher, Kristina. *Raising Racists: The Socialization of White Children in the Jim Crow South.* Lexington, KY: University of Kentucky Press, 2011.

Dye, Nancy S. and Noralee Frankel, eds. *Gender, Class, Race, and Reform in the Progressive Era.* Lexington, KY: University of Kentucky Press, 1991.

Edwards, Celestine, "Unity Our Aim," *Fratenity* 1 (1893): 1. Ellis, Mark. *Race, War, and Surveillance: African-Americans and the United States Government during World War II.* Bloomington, IN: Indiana University Press, 2001.

Ellis, Richard E. *The Union at Risk: Jacksonian Democracy, States' Rights, and the Nullification Crisis.* New York: Oxford University Press, 1989.

Emerson. Thomas I. and David Haber. *Political and Civil Rights in the United States.* Buffalo, NY: Dennis, 1952.

English, Ross M. *The United States Congress.* Manchester, England: Manchester University Press, 2003.

Feagin, Joe R., Hernán Vera, and Pinar Batur, *White Racism: The Basics*, 2nd ed. (New York: Routledge, 2001.

Feimster, Crystal. *Southern Horrors: Women and the Politics of Rape and Lynching.* Cambridge, MA: Harvard University Press, 2009.

Feldman, Glenn. *Politics, Society, and the Klan in Alabama, 1915-1949.* Tuscaloosa, AL: University of Alabama Press, 1999.

Fleming, Walter L. *Documentary History of Reconstruction: Political, Military, Social, Religious, Educational and Industrial 1865 to the Present Time.* Whitefish, MT: Kessinger Publishing, LLC, 2006.

"Filibuster Delays Anti-Lynching Bill." *New York Times*, January 5, 1922.

"Filibuster Ended As Senate Shelves Anti-Lynching Bill." *The New York Times,* February, 22, 1938.

Fischer, D. H. *Albion's Seed: Four British folkways in America.* New York: Oxford University Press, 1989.

Foner, Phillip and Robert James Branham, *Lift Every Voice: African American Oratory, 1787 – 1900.* Tuscaloosa, AL: University of Alabama Press, 1998.

Ford, William. "Constitutionality of Proposed Federal Anti-Lynching Legislation." *Virginia Law Review* 34 (1948): 944-53.

Francis, Professor Megan Ming. *Civil Rights and the Making of the Modern American State.* United Kingdom: Cambridge University Press, 2014.

Franklin, John Hope. *The Militant South.* Cambridge, Mass.: Harvard University Press, 1941.

Freedman, Estelle B. *Redefining Rape.* Cambridge, MA: Harvard University Press, 2013.

Frederickson, George M. *White Supremacy: A Comparative Study in American and South African History*. New York: Oxford University Press, 1981.

Gabbidon, Shaun L. and Helen Taylor Greene. *Race, Crime, and Justice: A Reader*. New York: Psychology Press, 2005.

Garb, Margaret. *Freedom's Ballot: African American Political Struggles in Chicago from Abolition to the Great Migration*. Chicago, IL: University Of Chicago Press, 2014.

Garner, James W. "New Politics for the South," *Annals of the American Academy of Political and Social Science* 35 (1910): 172-183.

Gerston, Larry N. *American Federalism: A Concise Introduction*. Armonk, NY: M.E. Sharpe, 2007.

Ginzburg, Ralph. *One Hundred Years of Lynching*. New York: Lancer Books, 1962.

Goduti, Jr., Philip A. *Robert F. Kennedy and the Shaping of Civil Rights, 1960-1964*. Jefferson, NC: McFarland, 2012.

Goff-Lightweis, Jennie. *Blood at the Root: Lynching as American Cultural Nucleus*. Albany, NY: SUNY Press, 2011.

Gordon, Jacob U. *Black Leadership for Social Change*. Westport, CT: Praeger, 2000.

Granucci, Anthony F. "Nor Cruel and Unusual Punishment Inflicted: The Original Meaning." *California Law Review* 57 (1969): 842.

Green, Robert P. Jr., ed. *Equal Protection and the African American Constitutional Experience: A Documentary History*. Westport, CT: Greenwood Press, 2000.

Gunning, Ann Arbor Sandra. *Race, Rape, and Lynching: The Red Record of American Literature, 1890-1912*. New York: Oxford University Press, 1996.

Guthrie, William D. *Lectures on the 14th Article of Amendment to the Constitution of the U.S.* New York: Da Capo Press, 1970.

Guzman, Jessie P. and W. Hardin Hughes, "Lynching Crime." *The Making of African American Identity* 3 (1917-1968): 9.

Hall, Jacquelyn Dowd. *Revolt against Chivalry: Jessie Daniel Ames and the Women's Campaign against Lynching*. New York: Columbia University Press, 1979.

Hale, Grace E. *Making Whiteness: The Culture of Segregation in the South, 1890-1940*. New York: Pantheon Books, 1998.

Hamm, Walter C. "The Three Phases of Colored Suffrage." *The North American Review* 168 (1899): 285-296.

Harper, Kimberly. *White Man's Heaven: The Lynching and Expulsion of Blacks in the Sothern Ozarks, 1894-1909*. Fayetteville, AR: University of Arkansas Press, 2010.

Harris, Trudier. *Exorcising Blackness: Historical and Literary Lynching and Burning Rituals*. Bloomington, IN: Indiana University Press, 1984.

Hart, Albert Bushnell. "The Outcome of the Southern Race Question." *The North American Review* 188 (1908): 50-61.

Hill, Karlos K. "Black Vigilantism: African American Lynch Mob Activity in the Mississippi and Arkansas Deltas, 1883-1923." *Journal of African American History* 95. 1 (2010): 26-43.

Hill, Rebecca N. *Men, Mobs, and Law: Anti-Lynching and Labor Defense in U.S. Radical History*. Durham, NC: Duke University Press, 2008.

Hine, Darlene Clark. and William C. Hine. and Stanley HaroldHsks. *The African-American Odyssey*. Upper Saddle River, NJ: Pearson, 2011.

Hixson, William B. Jr. *Moorfield Storey and the Abolitionist Tradition*. New York: Oxford University Press, 1972.

Hollars, B. J. *Thirteen Loops: Race, Violence, and the Last Lynching in America*. Tuscaloosa, AL: University of Alabama Press, 2011.

hooks, bell. *Killing Rage: Ending Racism (Owl Book)*. Reprint ed. New York: Holt Paperbacks, 1996.

Horwitz, Allan V. *The Logic of Social Control*. New York: Plenum Press, 1990.

Howard, George Elliott. "The Social Cost of Southern Race Prejudice." *American Journal of Sociology* 22 (1917): 577-593.

Hudson, Janet G. *Entangled by White Supremacy: Reform in World War I-Era South Carolina*. Lexington, KY: University Press of Kentucky, 2009.

Jack, Bryan M. *The St. Louis African American Community and the Exodusters.* Columbia: University of Missouri, 2008.

Jackson, Kenneth T. *The Ku Klux Klan in the City, 1915 – 1930.* New York: Oxford University Press, 1992.

James, Joseph B. *The Ratification of the Fourteenth Amendment.* Macon, GA: Mercer University Press, 1984.

James, Martin O. *Congressional Oversight.* New York: Nova Science, 2002.

January, Brendan. *Civil Rights.* Chicago: Heinemann, 2003.

Jelks, William Dorsey. "The Acuteness of the Negro Question: A Suggested Remedy." *The North American Review* 184 (1907): 389-395.

Katy, William. *Thirty Years of Lynching in the United States, 1889-1918.* New York: Negro Universities Press, 1969.

Kelley, Robin D. G., and Earl Lewis, eds. *To Make Our World Anew: Volume I: a History of African Americans to 1880.* New York: Oxford University Press, 2005.

Kennedy, David, M. *Over Here: The First World War and American Society.* New York: Oxford University Press, 1980.

Kirkpatrick, Jennet. *Uncivil Disobedience: Studies in Violence and Democratic Politics.* Princeton, NJ: Princeton University Press, 2008.

Klarman, Michael J. *From Jim Crow to Civil Rights: The Supreme Court and the Struggle for Racial Equality.* New York: Oxford University Press, 2004.

Klinkner, Philip A., and Rogers M. Smith. *The Unsteady March: the Rise and Decline of Racial Equality in America.* Chicago, IL: University of Chicago Press, 2002.

Kyvig, David E. *Daily Life in the United States, 1920-1940: How Americans Lived through the.* Chicago: Ivan R. Dee, 2004.

Lester, J.C and David Wilson. *Ku Klux Klan: Its Origin, Growth and Disbandment.* New York: AMS Press, 2010.

Liska, Allen E. ed. *Social Threat and Social Control.* Albany, NY: SUNY Press, 1992.

Litwack, Leon. "Hell Hounds." In *Without Sanctuary: Lynching Photography in America,* edited by James Allen. Santa Fe, NM: Twin Palms Press, 2000.

"Lynch Bill Faces Senate Filibuster." *The New York Times,* March 26, 1940.

"Lynchings in 1919," *The Literary Digest* 64 (1920): 20.

"Lynching is Unpatriotic." *The New York Times,* July 27, 1918.

MacLean, Nancy. "The Leo Frank Case Reconsidered: Gender and Sexual Politics in the Making of Reactionary Populism." *Journal of American History* 78 (1991): 917-48.

MacNeil, Neil. *Forge of Democracy: The House of Representatives.* New York: D. McKay, 1963.

Markovitz, Jonathan. *Legacies of Lynching: Racial Violence and Memory.* Minneapolis, MN: University of Minnesota Press, 2004.

Marshall-Browne, Gloria J. *Race, Law and American Society.* New York: Routledge, 2013.

Mathews, Donald G. "The Southern Rite of Human Sacrifice." *Journal of Southern Religion* 3 (2000): 1-36.

McClain, Emlin. "Constitutional Guarantees of Fundamental Rights." In *Modern American Law: A Systematic and Comprehensive Commentary on the Fundamental Principles of American Law and Procedure, Accompanied by Leading Illustrative Cases and Legal Forms with a Revised Edition of Blackstone's Commentaries,* edited by Eugene Allen Gilmore. Chicago, IL: Blackstone Institute, 1914.

McKinley, Albert E. "Two New Southern Constitutions." *Political Science Quarterly* 18 (1903): 480-511.

McMahan, Jeff. *The Ethics of Killing: Problems at the Margins of Life.* New York: Oxford University Press, 2003.

Miles, Robert and Malcolm Brown. *Racism.* 2nd ed. London: Routledge, 2003.

Morris, Aldon D. *Origins of the Civil Rights Movement.* New York: Free Press, 1984.

Moses, Norton H., comp. *Lynching and Vigilantism in the United States: An Annotated Bibliography.* Westport, CT: Greenwood Press, 1997.

Muhammad, Khalil Gibran. *The Condemnation of Blackness: Race, Crime, and the Making of Modern Urban America.* Cambridge: Harvard University Press, 2011.

Mullane, Deirdre. *Crossing the Danger Water: Three Hundred Years of African-American Writing*. New York: Random House, 1993.

Myers, Wm. Starr. "Some Present-Day Views of the Southern Race Problem." *The Sewanee Review* 21 (1913): 341-349.

Myrdal, Gunnar. *An American Dilemma: the Negro Problem and Modern Democracy*. New Brunswick, NJ: Transaction Publishers, 1996.

Neubeck, Kenneth J. and Noel A. Cazenave. *Welfare Racism: Playing the Race Card against America's Poor*. New York: Routledge, 2001.

Nevels, Cynthia Skove. *Lynching to Belong: Claiming Whiteness through Racial Violence*. College Station, TX: Texas A&M University Press, 2007.

Nisbett, Richard E. and Dov Cohen. *Culture of Honor: The Psychology of Violence in the South*. Boulder, CO: Westview Press, 1996.

Odum, Howard W. "Some Studies in the Negro Problems of the Southern States." *The Journal of Race Development* 6 (1915): 185-191.

Olgetree, Charles Jr., and Austin Sarat, *From Lynch Mob to Killing State*. New York: NYU Press, 2006.

Olson, Joel. *The Abolition of White Democracy*. Minneapolis, MN: University of Minnesota Press, 2004.

Page, Thomas Nelson. "The Lynching of Negroes: Its Cause and Its Prevention." *The North American Review* 178 (1904): 33-48.

Page, Thomas Walker. "Lynching and Race Relations in the South." *The North American Review* 206 (1917): 241-250.

Pfeifer, Michael J. *Rough Justice Lynching and American Society, 1874-1947*. Champagne, IL: University of Illinois Press, 2004.

Pillsbury, Albert. "A Brief Inquiry into a Federal Remedy for Lynching." *Harvard Law Review* 15 (1902): 707-13.

Pinar, William F. *The Gender of Racial Politics and Violence in America: Lynching, Prison Rape, and the Crisis of Masculinity*. New York: Peter Lang International Academic Publishers, 2001.

"President Denounces Lynching." *San Francisco Call*, August 10, 1903.

Proffit, Joseph Edwin. "Lynching: Its Cause and Cure." *The Yale Law Journal* 7 (1898): 264-267.

"Public Conduct Legislation: History of Anti-Lynching Legislation in Congress," *The Congressional Digest* 1 (1922): 10-15.

Quarles, Benjamin. *The Negro in the Making of America*. 3rd ed. New York: Touchstone, 1996.

Quarles, Charles L. *The Ku Klux Klan and Related American Racialist and Anti-Semitic Organizations: A History and Analysis*. Jefferson, NC: McFarland, 1999.

"Racism in Ulster: Troubles Hid Our Prejudice; Expert Says Peace Process Has Unmasked Our Deep-Rooted Hatred of Other Cultures." *The News Letter (Belfast, Northern Ireland)*, January 9, 2004.

"Racism: The Evil That's Not Lurking Round Every Corner; A Top Writer Puts a Social Problem in Perspective." *Daily Mail (London)*, February 26, 1999.

Rae, Nicol C. *Southern Democrats*. New York: Oxford University Press, 1994.

Raper, Arthur. *Southern Commission on the Study of Lynching. The Tragedy of Lynching*. Chapel Hill, NC: University of North Carolina Press, 1933.

Relations, Chicago Commission on Race. *The Negro in Chicago: a Study of Race Relations and a Race Riot*. Chicago, IL: Univ. Chicago Press, 1923.

"Remedies for Lynch Law," *The Sewanee Review* 8 (1900): 1-11.

Rice, Anne P. *Witnessing Lynching: American Writers Respond*. New Brunswick, NJ: Rutgers University Press, 2003.

Rieselbach, Leroy N. *Congressional Politics: The Evolving Legislative System*. 2nd ed. Boulder, CO: Westview Press, 1995.

Rodriguez, Junius P. *Slavery in the United States: A Social, Political, and Historical Encyclopedia, Vol. 2*. Santa Barbara, CA: ABC-CLIO, 2007.

Roosevelt, Theodore. "International Peace." *The Advocate of Peace (1894-1920)* 72 (1910), 146-147.

Rosser, Luther Z. "The Illegal Enforcement of Criminal Law." *The Virginia Law Register* 7 (1921): 569-586.

Royce, Josiah. "Race Questions and Prejudices." *International Journal of Ethics* 16 (1906): 265-288.

Rushdy, Ashraf H.A. *American Lynching*. New Haven, CT: Yale University Press, 2012.

Seagrave, Kerry. *Lynching of Women in the United States: The Recorded Cases, 1851-1946*. Jefferson, NC: McFarland, 2010.

Seligmann, Herbert J. "Protecting Southern Womanhood." *The Nation*, June 14, 1919.

"Senate Apologizes for Not Passing Anti-Lynching Laws." *Associated Press*, June 13, 2005.

"Senate Filibuster Hits Chicago Crime." *The New York Times,* January 13, 1938.

Scalia, Antonin. *A Matter of Interpretation: Federal Courts and the Law (University Center for Human Values)*. Edited by Amy Gutmann. Princeton, NJ: Princeton University Press, 1998.

Schneider, Mark R. *Boston Confronts Jim Crow, 1890-1920*. Boston: Northeastern, 1997.

Schwabe, William, Lois M. Davis, and Brian A. Jackson. *Challenges and Choices for Crime-Fighting Technology: Federal Support of State and Local Law Enforcement*. Santa Monica, CA: Rand, 2001.

Shafer, Byron E. and Richard Johnston, *The End of Southern Exceptionalism: Class, Race, and Partisan Change in the Postwar South*. Cambridge, MA: Harvard University Press, 2006.

Shapiro, Herbert. *White Violence and the Black Response: From Reconstruction to Montgomery*. Amherst, MA: University of Massachusetts Press. 1988.

Shay, Frank. *Judge Lynch, His First Hundred Years*. HP Publishing, 1938.

Short, James F. and Marvin E. Wolfgang, eds., *Collective Violence*. Chicago, IL: Aldine-Atherton, 1972.

Sims, Angela D. *Ethical Complications of Lynching: Ida B. Wells's Interrogation of American Terror*. New York: Palgrave Macmilllan, 2010.

Skowronek, Stephen, and Matthew Glassman, eds. *Formative Acts: American Politics in the Making*. Philadelphia: University of Pennsylvania Press, 2008.

Smead, Howard. *Blood Justice: The Lynching of Mack Charles Parker*. New York: Oxford University Press, 1988.

Smelser, Neil. *Theory of Collective Behavior*. London: Routledge & Kegan Paul, 1962.

Smith, J. Douglas. *Managing White Supremacy: Race, Politics, and Citizenship in Jim Crow Virginia*. Chapel Hill, NC: University of North Carolina Press, 2002.

Spierenburg, Petrus Cornelis. *Men and Violence: Gender, Honor, and Rituals in Modern Europe and America*. Columbus, OH: Ohio State University Press, 1998.

Steelwater, Eliza. *The Hangman's Knot: Lynching, Legal Execution, and America 's Struggle with the Death Penalty*. Boulder, CO: Westview Press, 2003.

Staton, John Roach. "Will Education Solve the Race Problem?" *The North American Review* 170 (1900): 785-801.

Stephenson, Gilbert Thomas. "Racial Distinctions in Southern Law." *The American Political Science Review* 1 (1906): 44-61.

Sutton, Robert P. *Federalism*. Westport, CT: Greenwood Publishing Group, 2002.

Tarr, G. Alan, Robert F. Williams, and Josef Marko, eds. *Federalism, Subnational Constitutions, and Minority Rights*. Westport, CT: Praeger, 2004.

Taylor, Andrew J. *Congress: A Performance Appraisal*. Boulder, CO: Westview Press, 2013.

Tillinghast, Joseph Alexander. "The Negro in Africa and America." *Publications of the American Economic Association* 3 (1902): 695-697.

"The House Debates the Dyer Anti-Lynching Bill," *The Congressional Digest* 1 (1922): 10-15.

Thurston, Robert W. *Lynching: American Mob Murder in Global Perspective*. Burlington, VT: Ashgate Publishing, 2011.

"Time to Understand What Is Racism and Unpack Genesis of the Phenomenon." *Cape Times (South Africa)*, November 3, 2009.

Tolnay, Stewart E., and E.M. Beck. *A Festival of Violence: An Analysis of Southern Lynchings, 1882 – 1930*. Champagne, IL: University of Illinois Press, 1995.

Tourgee, Albion. "A By-stander's Notes," *Anti-Caste* 5 (1892): 2.

Towns, W. Stuart. *Oratory and Rhetoric in the Nineteenth Century South: A Rhetoric of Defense*. Westport, CT: Praeger, 2000.

Trotman, C. James. *Frederick Douglass: a Biography (Greenwood Biographies)*. Santa Barbara, CA: Greenwood, 2011.

Tucker, John R. *The Constitution of the United States: A Critical Discussion of its Genesis, Development, and Interpretation*, edited by Henry St. George Tucker 2 vols. Chicago: Callaghan and Company, 1899.

United States Congressional Serial Set, Issue 7921. Nabu Press, 2012.

Vandal, Gilles. *Rethinking Southern Violence: Homicides in Post-Civil War Louisiana, 1866-1884*. The History of Crime and Criminal Justice Series. Columbus: Ohio State University Press, 2000.

Vandiver, Margaret. *Lethal Punishment*. New Brunswick, NJ: Rutgers University Press, 2006.

Vaughn, Victor C. "Crime and Disease." *Journal of the American Institute of Criminal Law and Criminology* 5 (1915): 688-694.

Wade, Wyn Craig. *The Fiery Cross: The Ku Klux Klan in America*. New York: Simon and Schuster, 1987.

Waldrep, Christopher. "National Policing, Lynching, and Constitutional Change." *Journal of Southern History* 74 (2008): 593.

Waller, James. *Face to Face: The Changing State of Racism across America*. New York: Insight Books, 1998.

Walston-Dunham, Beth. *Introduction to Law*. 6th ed. Clifton Park, NY: Cengage Learning, 2012.

Walter, David. "Legislative Notes and Reviews: Proposals for a Federal Anti-Lynching Law." *The American Political Science Review* 28 (1934): 436-42.

Ware, Vron. *Beyond the Pale: White Women, Racism and History*. London: Verso, 1992.

Wasniewski, Matthew, ed. *Black Americans in Congress, 1870-2007*. 3rd ed. Washington, D.C.: United States Congress, 2008.

Wasserstrom, Richard. "Federalism and Civil Rights by Burke Marshall." *The University of Chicago Law Review* 33 (1966): 407.

Watson, Charles. "Need of Federal Legislation in Respect to Mob Violence." *Yale Law Journal* 25 (1916): 561-81.

Wawro, Gregory J. and Eric Schickler. *Filibuster: Obstruction and Lawmaking in the U.S. Senate*. Princeton, NJ: Princeton University Press, 2013.

Weatherford, W. D. "Race Relationship in the South." *Annals of the American Academy of Political and Social Science* 49 (1913): 164-172.

Wells Barnett, Ida B. *Ida B. Wells on Lynching*. Amherst, NY: Humanity Books, 2002.

———. *Southern Horrors: Lynch Law in All Its Phases*. ReadHowYouWant, 2009.

West, Robin. *Progressive Constitutionalism: Reconstructing the Fourteenth Amendment*. Durham: Duke University Press Books, 1994.

White, Walter. *Rope and Faggot: A Biography of Judge Lynch*. New York: Arno Press, 1969.

Wilcox, W. F. "Is Race Friction between Blacks and Whites in the United States Growing and Inevitable?" *American Journal of Sociology* 13 (1908): 820-840,

Williams, Horace Randall, and Ben Beard. *This Day in Civil Rights History*. Montgomery, AL: NewSouth Books, 2009.

Williamson, Joel. *The Crucible of Race: Black and White Relations in the American South since Emancipation*. New York: Oxford University Press, 1984.

Wilson, Sondra Kathryn. *In Search of Democracy: The NAACP Writings of James Weldon Johnson, Walter White, and Roy Wilkins (1920-1977)*. New York: Oxford University Press, 1999.

Wilson, Woodrow. "The States and the Federal Government." *The North American Review* 187 (1908), 684-701.

Work, Monroe N. "Negro Criminality in the South." *Annals of the American Academy of Political and Social Science* 49 (1913): 74-80.

Wright, George C. *Racial Violence in Kentucky 1865 – 1940*. Baton Rouge, LA: Louisiana State University Press, 1990.

Wright, Gerald C., Jr., Leroy N. Rieselbach, and Lawrence C. Dodd, eds. *Congress and Policy Change*. New York: Agathon, 1986.

Zelleke, Andy. "The Politics of Language, *Identity, and Race the Rhetoric of Racism is Unfair to All U.S. Citizens, Poisoning the Atmosphere for Democratic Debate. " The Christian Science Monitor*, February 29, 1996.

Zimmerman, Joseph F. *Congress: Facilitator of State Action.* Albany: SUNY Press, 2010.

7/2/15